Praise for

"Long ago, I figured out that I would simply read whatever Bill Barich writes." **—Richard Ford**

"Bill Barich gets to the heart of the Irish pub, but he also gets to the soul of contemporary Ireland. At times it's through the glass darkly—as well it should be—and this book is never without wit or style or charm. Barich has got to be one of the most writerly pub goers around." **—Colum McCann, author of *Zoli* and *This Side of Brightness***

"Nicely researched, intelligently written, his book is a fun read tinged with melancholy at the thought of time passing and things changing; appropriately Irish, I think." **—*Minneapolis Star Tribune***

"Driven by a need to experience a timeless tavern like the one in John Ford's 1952 film 'The Quiet Man'—a place with a strong sense of community, where the art of conversation flourishes— Barich travels throughout Ireland and is routinely disappointed . . . Barich weaves a never-ending stream of oddly engaging historical and literary references into every dead end." **—*New York Times***

"Profound and perceptive . . . The Irish didn't invent the pub, says Barich, but made it their own, one of those 'third spaces' which is neither home nor workplace. Barich tells [his story] well, getting many characters to open up about their lives. In the process, he demolishes myths." **—*Irish Times***

"The American writer Bill Barich moved to Ranelagh, on Dublin's south side, some time ago and set out to find the perfect Irish pub. *A Pint of Plain* is an engaging account of his quest and investigations . . . In no time at all, Barich comes face to face with the horror that makes up a great deal of pub life in the New Ireland: loud piped pop music; amplified traditional-music sessions; gigantic, bar-dominating TVs; inept bar staff."

—Boston Globe

"Most browsers will pick this up because they want to read about Irish pubs, but they will get much, much more than they expected. An excellent, however sneaky, addition to the literature of globalization."   **—Booklist**

"The author wins us over with his delicious sense of humor, stylish storytelling and abundant affection for Ireland and its people."

—Kirkus Reviews

A PINT OF PLAIN

*Tradition, Change, and the
Fate of the Irish Pub*

Bill Barich

Skyhorse Publishing

Skyhorse Publishing books may be purchased in bulk at special discounts for sales promotion, corporate gifts, fund-raising, or educational purposes. Special editions can also be created to specifications. For details, contact the Special Sales Department, Skyhorse Publishing, 307 West 36th Street, 11th Floor, New York, NY 10018 or info@skyhorsepublishing.com.

Skyhorse® and Skyhorse Publishing® are registered trademarks of Skyhorse Publishing, Inc.®, a Delaware corporation.

Visit our website at www.skyhorsepublishing.com.

10 9 8 7 6 5 4 3 2 1

Library of Congress Cataloging-in-Publication Data is available on file.

Cover design by Tom Lau
Cover photo credit: Marcus Farrar

Print ISBN: 978-1-5107-3219-3
Ebook ISBN: 978-1-5107-3220-9

Printed in the United States of America.

For Imelda,
ever brighter

CONTENTS

Chapter 1

A PINT OF PLAIN

YOU COULD SAY my fascination with the Irish pub began long before I ever set foot in Ireland. Like so many other romantics, I was steeped in the allure of the country through the work of its great writers and musicians, and I thought of it as an enchanted land beyond the grip of change. I'd seen *The Quiet Man* far too many times, as well, and though I knew the movie was sentimental, filled with stereotypes, and deliberately unreal— a "beautiful travelogue," John Ford called it—I let it color my perceptions and felt compelled to start looking for a local as soon as I settled in Ranelagh, a neighborhood south of the Liffey, where I joined a lovely Dublin woman I had the good luck to meet on holiday in London and the good sense to follow home.

In my innocence, I assumed it would be easy to find a pub as devoutly Irish as Pat Cohan's in Cong, the village in County Mayo where *The Quiet Man* was filmed in 1951. The city might not deliver a whitewashed cottage with a thatched roof, of course, but surely there would be many bars where a sense of tradition prevailed, and a genial but hardnosed publican kept the intrusions and distractions of the civilized world at bay to allow the art of conversation to flourish. Ireland has about twelve thousand pubs to choose from, after all. Moreover, I'd been in training for the job most of my life, starting as a bored college student trapped in the snowbound wastes of upstate New York. Whenever my boredom peaked, I had one remedy only. I hitched a ride to Manhattan, wallowed in the beery charm of such iconic spots as McSorley's Old Ale House and P.J. Clarke's, and pretended I'd fetched up on the Auld Sod.

The word "Irish" soon acquired a special meaning for me. It stood for talk, drink, laughter, fun, and a release from ordinary cares. I found the literary angle appealing, too. As a secret poet, I hoped the beer would lift me into the realm of Yeatsian glory. The lines I scribbled on bar napkins certainly *seemed* to improve with each pint, and before long I couldn't pass even a lowly Blarney Stone without feeling a twitch of inspiration. That may sound ridiculous, but the Irish pub, at least in its mythic form, encourages such fantasies. Its attraction is universal, and it cuts across cultural boundaries and crops up everywhere on earth with a frequency matched only by the unavoidable Chinese restaurant. A plate of dim sum doesn't conjure images as seductive as the Lake Isle of Innisfree, though. For that you need a jar of the black stuff and Van Morrison on your iPod.

In my travels over the years, I gathered further evidence of the pub's enduring popularity. At an "Irish" bar in the Caribbean, I drank rum with a noted cricketer and discussed C. L. R. James, the sport's premier author, and at another in Florence I joined some fashionable Italians, all carrying shopping bags from the boutiques on Via Tornabuoni, in a fractured sing-along of "Danny Boy." The Fountain, once my local in Islington, North London, morphed into Filthy McNasty's, rumored to be a favorite pit stop of the Pogues' Shane MacGowan, an endorsement of Irishness money couldn't buy. I sampled stout in Malaga and Vancouver, Paris and Guadalajara, and became convinced that even if I journeyed to the far reaches of the globe, to São Tomé or the Trobriand Islands, I'd catch a glimpse of the familiar Guinness logo on the horizon.

My experience was so vast I considered myself a modest expert on the subject when I made the move to Dublin. It never occurred to me that the Clancy's and O'Malley's I'd visited elsewhere were mere imitations based on an ideal, or variations on a theme. A quick tour of the city taught me that the homegrown pubs exist in a bewildering array of styles now, from the architectural splendor of Doheny & Nesbitt to the grottolike confines of the Dawson Lounge, down a tricky staircase and into a cellar with only 350 square feet of space. Café en Seine was a temple of baroque overkill furnished with a hodge-podge of statuary, ferns, and sconces, while John Kehoe looked so unadorned that it scoffed at the very notion of decoration. From friends I heard about gay pubs, Polish and Nigerian pubs, early houses that opened at seven, and illicit after-hours pubs that supposedly never closed, but I stuck to my guns.

I wanted a local with a timeless quality. It should be humble and welcoming, I thought, and have a strong sense of community, where a shared set of values still obtained. The pub I imagined embodied the virtues traditionally associated with Ireland—kind and gentle, polite, good-humored, and devoted to the spoken word in all its base and exalted forms. It would be a refuge, a safe harbor with worn wood floors, a bar that could tell stories, gents in flat caps, and a turf fire blazing on cold winter nights. There I sat at a warm corner table with my Irish pals, a postmodern John Wayne basking in tranquility and relishing the sweet mood of surcease that Flann O'Brien described so memorably in "The Workmans Friend."

> When things go wrong and will not come right,
> Though you do the best you can,
> When life looks black as the hour of night—
> A PINT OF PLAIN IS YOUR ONLY MAN.
>
> When money's tight and is hard to get
> And your horse has also ran,
> When all you have is a heap of debt—
> A PINT OF PLAIN IS YOUR ONLY MAN.

I had no doubt I'd discover such a pub eventually. As I say, I was an innocent, and I still had a lot to learn.

Chapter 2

JACK BIRCHALL'S
RANELAGH HOUSE

M Y SEARCH FOR the perfect local started in Ranelagh, a bustling, prosperous neighborhood with the air of a tightly knit village. The oldest houses, built in terraces of brown and rust-colored brick, date from the 1760s, although most residences are of a later vintage, Victorian rather than Georgian. Palm trees grow in some gardens, a side effect of the temperate Gulf Stream, and the sight of them takes unsuspecting visitors by surprise. (The Irish climate isn't as harsh as it used to be, I've been told. Winters can be agreeable, but the cool, gray, bloodless summers are still tough on a former Californian.) Front doors are brightly painted, the iron gates and fences are constantly re-touched, and lace curtains still flutter in some windows. Although crime of any kind is rare, everyone has an alarm system, and they go off with spectacular regularity and grate on people's nerves.

Ranelagh Road, the main commercial strip, is just a block from our house. Until recently, you could walk there and buy a paper from a newsdealer who fancied the horses, pick up some vegetables at the greengrocer's, and stop at a butcher shop for some lamb chops for the evening meal, but you can't do it anymore. The small tradesmen have disappeared, driven out by whopping real estate prices and the inability to compete with supermarkets and franchised convenience stores. Ranelagh's terraces may look plain and uniform from the outside, but the new money spills over into the streets, where a fleet of shiny Range Rovers, Mercedes, and BMWs vie for attention and status. Once you could only order the most basic fare at our restaurants—glorified chip shops, actually—but now you can dine on foie gras and prune terrine with pear puree, pickled pear slices, and pistachio oil at a bistro with a Michelin star.

All that's left of the old Ireland, really, are two bookie joints and eight pubs of varying character. Six of the pubs are on Ranelagh Road, separated by only two hundred yards. It's difficult to see how they can survive in such close proximity, but the Irish have always been overstocked with licensed premises. A survey done in 1635 counted 1,189 merchants selling ale and whiskey (*uisce beatha* in Gaelic, or "water of life") to the roughly four thousand families who lived in Dublin, while folks in the country were even better served. As late as 1924, the Committee on Intoxicating Liquor cited boozy enclaves like Ballymore in County Sligo, where 27 of 200 houses held a license; the hamlet of Gurteen (6 of 15 houses); and Blacklion in County Cavan, where the tally was 8 of 20 houses.

The Hill struck me as Ranelagh's most eye-catching pub, so I tried it first. Founded in 1845, it occupies a knoll on the fringe of the village and has a canary-yellow paint job that flashes like a beacon on gloomy, overcast afternoons. Off the beaten track, it doesn't attract many outsiders, and its stalwart regulars give it an

inbred quality a stranger—or a "blow-in," as the Irish put it—
might have trouble cracking. I felt more comfortable at Corrigan's
Mount Pleasant Inn around the corner, a forthright, unpretentious
spot. It was as if I'd wandered into the parlor of somebody's
maiden aunt, where the upholstery was slightly faded and a long-
haired cat, invisible yet somehow present, was on the prowl. Corrigan's made you want to curl up for a nap, maybe removing your
shoes and socks in the process, but the TV, tuned to Sky News, a
cable network that recycles the same stories for hours—there was
no TV at Pat Cohan's—was a minor nuisance, plus the Mount
Pleasant area was just a little too far from home to be practical on
a stormy night.

Next I turned to the pubs on Ranelagh Road, where I ruled
out Russells right away. On some weekends, it functioned as a
singles bar with burly bouncers in black at the door, and that
caused me to suffer California flashbacks. Santa Monica belongs
in Santa Monica, not Dublin—that was my attitude. Whenever
I strolled past Russells on a frigid evening in the so-called Irish
summer, my heart went out to the young women waiting in line,
who shivered in skimpy dresses intended for a balmy beach town
and showed off their Fake Bake tans. They could have taken
shelter at the Four Provinces nearby, but I understood their reluctance. The Four Provinces (gone now, bought by a supermarket
chain along with its license to sell alcohol) was both cavernous and
anonymous, no more cozy than a bus station fed by a steady stream
of transients. In my single visit, I could feel plots being hatched
and ill-advised liaisons about to burst into flame, so I crossed it off
my short list.

I explored Smyths and T. Humphreys, Grocer more thoroughly.

The pubs are adjacent to each other, so a customer is never far from redemption. If you play the fool at Smyths and get the boot, you're only steps away from an unblemished record and a fresh pint at Humphreys, where a big front window allows pedestrians to observe the drinkers inside. Most pubs block their windows with panels of leaded or stained glass, or just shades or shutters, to guarantee privacy, and that leads to a trove of folklore among abstainers about the goings-on behind closed doors. (Two bridges over the Liffey are named in honor of temperance advocates, in fact.) Smyths was very efficient and well run, and the "pub grub" could be excellent, but the place carried a hint of the sports bar and also depended on recorded music to create an atmosphere— there was no recorded music at Pat Cohan's, only impromptu song—while Humphreys, though nice enough, never affected me one way or another.

That left only two pubs to consider, just ten yards apart—Jack Birchall's Ranelagh House and R. McSorley & Sons, no relation to the renowned watering hole of my youth. I peeked into Mc-Sorley's first and was captivated. Like Humphreys, the pub had once sold groceries and sundries as well as alcohol, and it retained a musty dignity that spoke of permanence. An antique apothecary's cabinet was on display, its drawers labeled "iodine" and "oil of camphor," while a penny-farthing bike collected dust by some scruffy church pews probably bought for a pittance at a rummage sale. I enjoyed the eclectic flavor and the haphazard charm, and interpreted the apparently random accumulation of bric-a-brac as a symbol of the genuine. That's what I craved, after all—some contact with the authentic, that soulful Ireland of legend.

At McSorley's, I established myself as a two-pint man, referring to the number of beers I consumed at a sitting, although the figure wasn't carved in stone and I surpassed it at times, always to my detriment. An Irish poet had alerted me to this token of identity when we met by chance at a B and B in West Cork. He was working on an autobiography and asked if I'd help him recall the spots where he might have hung out as a visiting professor in the Bay Area many years ago. I was happy to oblige and listed the prime suspects near City Lights Books—Vesuvio, Tosca, Grant & Green, then a chow mein overdose at New Woey Loy Goey—although my participation cast the art of the memoir in a new light. The poet swore he was a three-pint man—about average, I'd guess, based on casual observation—but not a performance that would rattle any of Dublin's truly heroic pintmen, whose hollow legs are the stuff of myth.

Quality matters as much as quantity to such serious topers as Tommy Lusty, who once testified to Kevin Kearns, a splendid oral historian of Dublin's street life. "Dooley's, that was one of the most famous pubs around when I started drinking about 1935," Lusty began, warming to his story. "Now there was plenty of other pints along the quay, but *that* pint, I'll tell you, it was always perfect. Oh, what a drink! They had one of the best cellars in Dublin. Pulled from the barrel down below, and you could *feel* the substance of it. And *no rush*. It might take ten minutes to bring it to a head, the cream. Oh, lovely. You could drink about twenty of them and the next morning you'd be like a two-year-old, there'd be no hangover."

Often I envy the talents of others, but I didn't envy Tommy Lusty despite his obvious pride in his gift. The idea of twenty pints of stout burbling through my system was enough to strangle any notions I might have harbored about becoming a truly heroic pintman myself. Content with my modest lot, I fell into the habit of visiting McSorley's in the early evening, when the pub was still calm and quiet and conducive to reading or meditation. "If you study the good pintman," mused Tom Corkery, another of Kearns's informants, "you will observe how he can stand staring into the glass for long periods, thinking deep thoughts." Corkery was correct up to a point, but he went overboard when he added, "This is because he knows the truth lies at the bottom of the glass." All I ever saw down there was some brindled foam.

At any rate, I adjourned to McSorley's at the cocktail hour two or three times a week. I couldn't call myself a regular since my commitment was not absolute. Such bonds are forged for life, barring bad behavior or an accident of fate, so I failed to command the same barstool or chair I'd grabbed the day before, and the day before that, on into eternity. I could plant myself anywhere, really, because the crowd didn't materialize until much later. Many of the Irish avoid the pub until after dinner, a sound strategy for promoting relative sobriety, and they roll in about eight or nine o'clock, with their numbers increasing exponentially as closing time draws near at eleven thirty. Some pubs, McSorley's among them, purchase special late-night exemptions that let them serve drinks until two A.M. on Thursday, Friday, and Saturday, and they're often packed with revelers—little wonder, then, that the average price of a Dublin pub in a decent location is about seven million dollars.

I never had the nerve to ask Kevin Hynes what he and his partner, an investor from Arklow, paid for R. McSorley & Sons.

(Some Irish pubs keep the name of the original licensee.) The deal, done in private, took me by surprise. There were no "For Sale" signs posted, no gossip or rumors to tip me off in advance. Just as I'd begun to eye a particular stool and covet it as my seat, destiny kicked it out from under me, and I felt cheated. There was more bad news, too—the owners planned to redecorate. The pub might look full on Saturday night, Kevin once explained to me, but business was slow in general. McSorley's required a complete makeover, and that's what it got. When it reopened, it resembled a swanky gentlemen's club in dark wood and leather, with a lounge bar spacious enough for a DJ and a dance floor. Again, I thought of America—of New York City's slick Upper East Side. I missed the bric-a-brac, that symbol of the genuine.

Kevin set me straight. The bric-a-brac was phony. A designer had sourced it from various suppliers to manufacture a nostalgic, traditional atmosphere. The bicycle and the church pews were junk, worthless, no more than stage props. Had they been authentic antiques, Kevin might have saved them. He's canny, engaging, and in his thirties, one of ten children and a son of Dessie Hynes, an eminent publican who's now retired. Dessie owned several pubs in Dublin and put Kevin to work as a teenager to teach him the trade. Later Kevin emigrated to the U.S. and ran some Irish bars in Manhattan, and though he loved the flash and the speed of the Big Apple, he returned home to be closer to his aging parents, though he vowed to be a New Yorker again some day soon.

Hynes's time abroad had influenced his decision to redo McSorley's. The market demanded an elegant, modern, sophisticated pub, he believed, where the customers could socialize in a classy environment that appealed to both sexes. The days when a publican could rely on a slew of hard-core boozers to pay the mortage were gone, along with the spittoons and the sawdust on the floor. Long ago, in an era of oppressive tenements and widespread poverty, some men knew no other type of entertainment and spent every last penny on drink, regardless of their family obligations.

"They streamed in every morning and never left," Kevin recalled. "At closing time, we had to flick the lights and shout at them to leave. If they complained about a pint, we shoved them out the door. When I get a complaint now, I pass it on to the brewery. It's a whole different ball game."

The competition among pubs is fierce, he went on, not only in Ranelagh but all over the city, and they're up against attractions that Ireland never had in such abundance before—fine restaurants and cafés, elaborate movie complexes, dramatic shopping malls, and even Starbucks, along with video stores and the Internet. Budget airlines also take a toll. For the cost of a few pints, you can practically book a cheap flight to London. To combat the tide, Kevin dreams up gimmicks. He sponsors trivia nights with prizes, and hosts an annual Super Bowl bash. He also rents his lounge for birthday parties, often a thirtieth, the mean age of his clientele. When the pub closes, he picks up discarded tram tickets to see where people come from, so he can target them with ads and promotions. He distributes his business card to the neighbors and urges them to phone him instead of the cops when they have a problem. If a pipe bursts in a toilet, he fixes it himself. He likes doing repairs, he said, because it keeps him busy, but it sounded as if he already had plenty on his plate.

I commiserated with Kevin. Almost everybody wishes their job was a little easier. I definitely wished writing was easier. It was the illusion of ease that had drawn me to writing, back in my bored college days. "It looks easy," Auden once said in an interview I'd read, and I failed to hear the irony. Your ideas on a piece of paper, a lashing of drama or heartbreak, a cliffhanger ending—never mind the thirty years of solitary confinement and the damage to your brain. They don't mention those side effects in writing programs. Anyway, I hoped Kevin earned a fortune for his hard work, but the revamped McSorley's was too trendy to suit me. While the Irish publicans were racing toward the future and copying America—here was an irony I did appreciate—I, the wandering American, was dead set on embracing the traditional Irish pub, unspoiled and undoctored, before it vanished for good, so I transferred my affection to Jack Birchall's Ranelagh House.

I remember my first visit to Birchall's quite well. I'd just finished a not-so-easy stint of writing and decided to go for a walk to clear my head, feeling tired and eager for some company. When I reached the pub, I stopped outside to study the inscription in Latin on the stained-glass panels over its windows—*Quare Verum*, or Seek the Truth. How appropriate, I thought, wondering if Jack Birchall had been educated by the Jesuits. The inscription could also be translated as "No Bullshit Allowed," I later realized, since the pub's central motif was its simplicity, even humility. I was drawn toward the hearthlike glow pulsing through the stained glass, as radiant as a last blast of sunshine at twilight, and when I heard the warm babble of voices and the heady clink of glasses, I knew the craic would be mighty inside.

Craic looks as if it's an old Gaelic word, but it derives from the Anglo-Saxon. Pronounced "crack," it was spelled that way until the media recast it, *faux* style, to avoid any confusion with crack cocaine. At its most basic, it means fun, especially the fun to be had in pubs. Craic can be as elusive and free-floating as ectoplasm, suddenly appearing out of nowhere. The sociologist Adrian Peace has called it a "collectively produced performance." In the village of "Inverest"—not its real name—Peace recorded how the craic descended randomly on one pub. "Word spreads that the atmosphere is promising," he wrote. "People begin to drift in its direction . . . Conversation becomes intense, the noise level soars." Everyone enjoys the fun, but nobody can account for why it occurred at that particular pub on that particular night.

I followed the flow of the craic through a scuffed entryway and into a compact L-shaped room already crowded and brimming with good vibes. The size of the pub enhanced its bonhomie. You had to brush shoulders with someone just to buy a drink, an ideal pretext for a chat. The room had a pleasing lack of affectation, too. The décor was as abrupt as an afterthought, and the bric-a-brac truly had collected over time. Nobody would choose the stuff for its cuteness—a few vintage beer bottles on a shelf, say, and a tin that once held potato chips. On the walls were some landscapes in oil, including a portrait of swans on the Grand Canal; some faded photographs of unidentified persons; and a framed thank-you note for a donation to Guide Dogs for the Blind.

Upholstered banquettes offered comfortable seating, each with a table and some little stools about two feet high, perfect for a milkmaid. Normal stools lined the worn bar, divided into two sections by an arched doorway. At the back bar, solitary men were doing crossword puzzles or reading the paper, oblivious of the barely audible recorded music playing through hidden speakers. The front bar, where I ordered a pint of Guinness, was the epicenter of the craic. A barman, neatly dressed in a shirt and tie, filled a glass to the three-quarters mark and put it on a rubber mat to settle. I watched it froth and foam, agreeing with Tom Corkery. The mechanics and metaphysics of stout do promote contemplation.

Were the bubbles rising or falling? How long before the barman topped up the glass? Is Guinness really good for you, as the company's ads used to claim in the old days? The answer is, "Maybe," at least in moderation. The yeast residue contains traces of thirteen vitamins, while humulone, a chemical compound in the hops, has a mildly sedative effect. (Pillows stuffed with hops were once prescribed for insomniacs.) Whether stout acts as a tonic for "rundown" patients—a potential benefit the company once touted—is debatable, but some doctors still recommend it to nursing mothers to help them relax. Guinness has also been sold as a balm to invalids; a method for enriching iron-poor blood; a boost for a depressed appetite; and a calmative for the shattered nerves of those who are "weak and shaky."

Guinness tastes much better in Ireland than anywhere else, and you can buy a version of it in about 150 countries worldwide. The flavor of stout seems to change depending on where it's brewed. A pint in London doesn't have the same full-bodied, creamy richness of a Dublin pint—indeed, some London pubs now feature Guinness imported from Ireland—while the stout I drank in California struck me as a miserly imitation, thin and bitter and barely palatable in my opinion. Irish Guinness does have a drawback, though. It weighs heavily on the belly, more from its sheer heft and bulk than its alcoholic content, a relatively low 4.1–4.3 percent compared to 5.2 for Stella Artois, a popular Belgian lager. Dubliners refer to it as "liquid bread" or a "meal in a glass," even though a pint contains just 198 calories, less than a low-fat pint of milk.

Still, it takes some effort to swallow enough of it to attain the fuzzy state accurately described as "well-jarred." The more likely result of overindulgence will be soporific, as Charles Halliday noted in *An Inquiry Into the Influence of Spiritous Liquors in Producing Crime, Disease, and Poverty in Ireland*, published in 1830. Halliday argued that whiskey, not beer, was the problem. Even a single dram could rouse a drinker to the "highest pitch of animal excitement . . . mad for the commission of every type of villainy which his depraved imagination may suggest," but beer was benign and blameless. "To drink a quart of Ale or Porter requires some time, and there are few stomachs able to bear the quantity sufficient to produce intoxication, without allowing a considerable period to elapse, and the certain progress from drowsiness to stupor, which in the interval takes place, gradually renders harmless the wretched object deprived of reason."

As I nursed my second pint, I witnessed Adrian Peace's formula in action. People kept streaming through the door, possibly deserters from Russells or T. Humphreys who'd been sucked into the vortex, and the craic continued to mount. Customers were three deep at the front bar now, while the crossword puzzlers at the back bar had put down their pencils to converse with each another. Voices grew louder, as Peace had predicted, and the entire room seemed bathed in rosy light. The Irish may consume more alcohol per capita than any developed nation except Luxembourg, but its effects are modulated in a well-managed traditional pub. The staggering drunks who flooded Dublin's streets in Halliday's time are rare, and when you do see one, it's usually a young binge drinker reeling out of a nightclub in the wee hours.

Jack Birchall wouldn't tolerate any binges on his premises, anyway. He looked a commanding presence, as eagle-eyed as a ship's captain navigating a choppy sea and on the alert for a troublesome wave. Impeccably groomed, with the trace of a golf-course tan even in winter, he operated on the "firm but fair" principle, and the pub echoed his character. He supervised every detail and bent over backward to deal with his crusty regulars, who were the crustiest in Ranelagh by far. That he handled their idiosyncracies with good grace showed his devotion to his profession, one he was still practicing well into his seventies. He saw the publican's life as an honorable calling, I believe, and that made his patrons respect him. With Jack on duty, everyone drank responsibly because it would have been embarrassing to do otherwise.

He was a private man, who never engaged in happy talk. When I asked about his background once, he acted both gruff and shy. "Ah, you wouldn't want to be writin' about me," he objected. Born on a farm in County Kildare, he came to Dublin in his youth and latched on at a pub, where he spent six years as an apprentice and junior barman before he earned his stripes. The discipline was essential, he felt, and largely missing from many pubs today. For publicans, the system had advantages, since they paid their lads a menial wage. The lads put up with it because they shared a common goal. If they lived cheaply and saved, they might buy a pub some day with the help of a backer. That's difficult to accomplish now. Most pubs are too expensive, so being a barman isn't necessarily a step toward a brighter future. An old saying has it that you'll never attend a barman's funeral, because they run their own place eventually or quit the business for something better.

For Jack Birchall, the toil and the long hours paid off. He bought his first pub in the Liberties, so-called because the district lay beyond the jurisdiction of the medieval city. The Liberties has a rough-and-tumble history, fraught with bloodshed during the eighteenth century when a feud erupted between its Protestant tailors and weavers and the Catholic butchers at Ormond Market, who traded on the Liffey's north side. The butchers hacked at the Protestants' legs and severed their tendons; the Protestants retaliated by impaling the butchers on their own meat hooks. The Liberties was desperately poor in those days, as James Johnson, an American doctor, commented in 1844. "Winds and rain have *liberty* to enter freely through the windows of half the houses—the pigs have *liberty* to ramble about—the landlord has *liberty* to take possession of most of his tenements—the silk weaver has *liberty* to starve or beg."

By the time Jack set up shop, the Liberties, though still tough, had a solid blue-collar population. He made a success of that first pub and parlayed it into a more valuable one in Ranelagh, relying on a clever leapfrog scheme that compounded his original investment in real estate. McCauley's, the pub he acquired, once figured in the column Myles na gCopaleen wrote for the *Irish Times*. (Myles was really Brian O'Nolan, whose other literary alias was Flann O'Brien.) Having stopped at the pub for a pint of plain porter, the drink he praised in his doggerel, Myles became exercised about McCauley's clock. It only had one hand, he insisted, and he took a photo of the "seditious timepiece" to prove it, exhibiting it to his friends as evidence. The parlor trick worked until someone pointed out that the clock read 4:22, the hour when its hands overlap.

I heard about the leapfrog scheme from Dessie Hynes, Kevin's father, a dapper little man of eighty, who was a master at it. When we met at McSorley's, Dessie looked as if he could still perform a spritely tap dance. He came equipped with a file of clippings he thought might interest me. The McCranns, his mother's relatives, had owned some bars in Manhattan, and he produced a photo of their Gramercy Inn, where you dialed MUrray Hill 4-9153 for a reservation. Also in the file were a photo of the memorial statue atop the grave of Thomas McCrann (1875–1925), a former New Jersey state senator buried in Paterson, and an obituary notice for his wife Frances, who died at ninety-four. Last but not least, an article from the *Galway Advertiser* trumpeted the feats of Tommy Hynes, Dessie's uncle, who won the Irish Junior Cross Country Championship in 1901.

Dessie has the gift of gab. He lost his mother to tuberculosis when he was just eleven and went to live with his grandfather in rural Longford, where he failed to "absorb education" and instead fished in the Shannon River and rolled up reeds to smoke on its banks. At fourteen, he bolted for Dublin for the same reason Jack Birchall did, hoping to be hired at a pub even though he feared alcohol because of the damage it had done to some family members—he didn't take a drink himself until he was forty-five—but he was judged to be too small to lift the heavy kegs. "I'm the right size for a jockey," he laughed. He had the same problem in England, where he lodged with an aunt in Birmingham and

decided after ten days—and a taste of bangers and horsemeat—
that the country wasn't for him, so he returned to Longford,
worked at his uncle's dance hall, and opened a "picture show."

Always keen to improve his lot in life and seize an opportunity,
Dessie tried his hand at various other businesses, too. He sold
sweets from a van and drove the back roads like a madman, convinced he'd be dead before he turned thirty; distributed bread
with a similar disregard for the cattle and chickens that crossed
his path; owned an ice cream franchise; and purchased a main-
street shop, where he tripled the sales in just six weeks and later
sold it, giving him the seed money to move his family, nine children and counting, to the seaside suburb of Blackrock outside
Dublin, where he took over the Three Ton pub. This would form
the foundation of an empire as Dessie jumped from one pub to
the next, each worth more than its predecessor in an era before
capital gains taxes, until he picked up O'Donoghue's, his crowning
glory, in 1977, a "trophy pub" on Lower Baggot Street renowned
as a venue for folk music.

Everybody in Dublin knows O'Donoghue's. Apart from the
music, its trophy status derives from a choice location five minutes from Stephen's Green, and to the healthy income it gener-
ates by catering to a mix of tourists and locals. The pub's interior
is nothing to brag about, though. At O'Donoghue's, you feel as if
you've stumbled into a farmer's barn. It has a hayseed ruggedness
that complements the fiddles and guitars. Fans from around the
world honor it as the birthplace of the Dubliners, a notoriously
hard-living folk group, who began by performing for drinks at
the pub. The group's first big hit in Britain was "Seven Drunken
Nights," and you wouldn't be wrong to guess it carried an ele-

ment of autobiography. In photos, the Dubliners often glower at the camera with baleful intent, all wearing long, scraggly, anarchic beards like itinerant preachers of the apocalypse.

When Dessie assumed control, he realized in an instant why the pub had been struggling and was for sale. Musicians filtered in with their guitar, banjo, and fiddle cases and expected free booze, whether or not they were on the bill. He counted forty-three scroungers on his very first night. "It was like the St. Valentine's Day Massacre with all those fellas coming in," he told me, and he'd have been the unfortunate victim if he hadn't changed the house policy. He kept O'Donoghue's for about twelve years and built it back up, then moved a final time to Hynes (currently the Wellington) at Baggot Street Bridge, a pub notable for its fire-engine-red façade; the five grinning pints of stout and big clock ("It's Guinness Time!") on it; and the government workers and politicians from the Dail, or Parliament, nearby, who swapped views with Dessie over the critical issues.

I asked Dessie what made for a good publican. "Seeing people, being fond of people," he replied, without hesitation. In a sense, he took care of his flock. Barmen are called curates sometimes, because their duties are similar to a priest's. They preside over the celebrations at christenings, weddings, and wakes, and some of them even doubled as undertakers in the old days. Dessie extended credit to trustworthy customers and doled out an occasional loan. He offered advice if it was solicited, and might even drive a regular home on a rainy night. It's been said that a publican must be a democrat, an autocrat, an acrobat, and a doormat, and Dessie would agree. "Don't do this job if you don't like it," he warned. "Because if you like it, it *is* your life. I miss it, but I wouldn't be able for it anymore."

As for traditional pubs, Dessie steered me toward a fine one in Roscommon, where a relative of the owner had lost a fortune betting on horses and greyhounds. He also mentioned Lamb Doyles in the Dublin Mountains, only a few miles from the city. Sheep ranchers used to drink there, he said, and he remembered a man who ordered a baby brandy every afternoon and applied a splash of it to the lips of any lamb in distress. Dessie wrote his phone number in my notebook and invited me on a tour of the pubs in Rosslare, County Wexford, where he and his wife had retired, and I might have accepted if he hadn't spun all those tales about his madcap speeding and the near-collisions with animals. I thanked him, anyway, as he left to join Kevin and another son at the bar. "Ten pubs would have been better than ten kids," he quipped, but only a fool would believe him.

Chapter 3

A SHOCK TO THE SYSTEM

J ACK BIRCHALL'S RANELAGH House marked the end of
the trail. I adopted it as my local, ready to play by the unwrit-
ten rules. "Traditional Lounge," it said over the front door, a
boast the pub mostly fulfilled. True, Birchall's had recorded music, but it was never too loud, nor did it subject us to the likes of
Britney Spears. The TV, a boxy old console, rested on a high
ledge and only coughed itself to life for a major sporting event,
or an important news program such as the annual report on the
Irish budget, always a matter of concern because of a possible tax
hike on the price of a pint. Though the two fires were electric,
not turf, they kept us warm. The barmen were rock-steady and
dedicated to Jack, who'd tutored them well and exercised a control over the place that was somehow both iron-fisted and as light
as a feather.

As a budding regular, I gradually became aware of how much
effort goes into the upkeep of a first-rate pub. It reflected a con-
scientious attitude toward service, as well as a desire to preserve
and protect a costly piece of real estate. The attention to detail
was extraordinary. Every morning without fail, a staff member

polished the brass ledges below the windows outside, rubbing away all the smudges and fingerprints to restore a burnished glow. The colorful petunias that spilled from hanging planters needed to be watered, while the lunch specials had to be chalked on a blackboard and vetted, not always successfully. Along with greengrocers, who may earn an even lower grade—*turnups*, *carots*, I've seen them all—some pub employees wrestle with their spelling.

The kitchen at Birchall's dished up standard belly-busting fare rather than the effete wraps and panini featured on more *au courant* menus. Boiled bacon with parsley sauce, shepherd's pie, chicken curry, and the peculiar combo of lasagna and chips were the staples. Irish pubs didn't start cooking full meals until about twenty years ago—and some still don't, especially in the country, where a publican might glare at you if you ask for a bite to eat—but food represents a significant part of the business around Dublin. At Smyths, where both lunch and dinner are served, it constitutes about 30 percent of the gross receipts, but Birchall's lagged far behind, perhaps because the customers were so single-minded about their purpose—talk and drink, that is—and so set in their ways.

Once the brasses were polished, the pub's interior required some attention. The bare floors of wood and slate had to be mopped, the bottles and shelves were dusted, and a barman ran a vacuum over the carpeted areas. (The different floor surfaces, installed in different periods, contributed to Birchall's cobbled-together look. The pub hadn't been designed in advance, just added on to, and that was part of its charm.) Emptying a score of ashtrays used to be a nasty aspect of the ritual, but that stopped when a ban on smoking took effect in 2004. The ban had hurt some pubs, particularly "landlocked" ones in the inner city with no outdoor space. Smokers were bothered by the inconvenience, and many of them didn't want to announce their presence at a bar by standing in front of it for a cigarette. Smyths had room in back for a "beer garden," though, with patio heaters and picnic tables, and saw its profits increase. For barmen, the ban was a blessing. Liberated from the clouds of second-hand smoke, they felt healthier, brighter, and much more energetic.

Birchall's was so neat, spotless, and odorless by ten thirty, the opening hour, you might imagine the pub had hosted a dowager's tea party the night before. The petty griefs, the awkward flirtations, the loudmouth who insisted Italy rather than Brazil had won the World Cup in 1994 and knocked over his beer, they'd all been erased. This diligent act of erasure amounted to a canny psychological ploy. When the cops drag a criminal back to the scene of the crime, his fondest wish is that there won't *be* any scene, just a miracle whereby the evidence has vanished and left instead an antiseptic motel room or a forest glen absent of malice. It's the same with pubs. If you misbehave—and the odds are that you might— you don't care to be reminded of your orneriness on your next visit. It's much nicer to walk into an obsessively hygenic local and pretend the slate is clean again.

During the week, Birchall's is as quiet as a chapel until the lunch hour, and nearly as quiet after that. From the depths of Ranelagh, a straggly, fuzzy-tongued loner might emerge in search of some hair of the dog, but the first regulars don't arrive before the early evening. All-day drinkers of the Tommy Lusty school are few and far between, because many of the Irish have good jobs and fat salaries—and even fatter mortgages and bills to pay. They can't afford to slack off, and when they do drink, they frequently do it at home. The sale of wine has skyrocketed at off-licenses, or stores permitted to sell alcoholic beverages for consumption *off* the premises. Wine commands 21 percent of the market now, while the discount beer available at supermarkets—beer makes up only half the market at present, down from 69 percent in 1986—is much cheaper than a pint at the pub.

If you want to see the last of the early-morning drinkers, you have to visit a pub such as Ned's of Townsend Street, not far from the Liffey. Built in 1861, Ned's has a long history and an old custom of inviting valued employees to inscribe their names on a beam in the cellar. As an early house, it holds a license that allows it to open at seven A.M. to serve people "following the trade of their calling," originally dock workers on the quays along the river. Some dockers still come in, but the port's high-tech now, so they're technicians, not laborers, and they're joined by others who work a night shift—cabbies, pressmen from the *Irish Times*, bakers who often bring a box of rolls or buns fresh from the oven. There's a fair contingent of the neighborhood's elderly, too, who like to savor their drinks while the city's half-asleep and the threats that they fear, real or imagined, are dormant. They play cards, read the paper, and vanish before noon.

By all accounts, the dockers of yore were the most truly heroic pintmen Dublin has ever known. When you read about their exploits, you become a little dizzy yourself. A docker might start with a couple of pints even before he hoisted a crate or a steamer trunk, then take a break for a pint or two at ten o'clock, the "beero hour," and toss down another ration of suds with his lunch at home. Needless to say, he was still thirsty at quitting time and marched right back to the pub, where he communed with his brethren until the exhausted and probably relieved publican shut down. Oddly, some dockers had a bias against whiskey drinkers. They poked fun at their red faces and accused the men of being "culchies," or rubes fresh off the farm.

As I did at McSorley's, I liked to drop by Birchall's around six o'clock. A dozen or so suspects were usually deployed around the room, divided evenly between those who had just left the office and those who no longer had one, gents in their seventies who were the most punctual regulars by far. Due to their undeniable seniority, they could be both proprietary and territorial, advising Jack on questions of policy and glancing up with a sharp crick of the neck whenever the door swung open. If they recognized a familiar face, they were quick with a nod and a hello, but a stranger provoked scant curiosity. They drank Guinness, of course, because they'd been weaned on it, but stout only accounts for about 45 percent of the beer sold in Dublin pubs now, or the same amount as lager, with such brands as Bud and Coors Light currently in fashion. Hard cider, wine, and spirits account for the other 10 percent.

At first I was thrown off stride when a barman greeted me by asking, "Are you okay?" I thought I must look sickly or otherwise in distress, but the question only meant, "What would you like to drink?" implying that you couldn't be okay, not really, until you named your poison. I also had some difficulty adapting to the level of service. It was too good—unobtrusive, polite, discreet. No matter where I sat, the barman brought the pint to my table and refused to accept a tip. That's customary, but it still took some getting used to. I'd distributed a small fortune to American bartenders just for popping the cap on a beer bottle.

Once I *was* okay, I tried to avoid getting caught at the craic-heavy front bar, where it's almost impossible to avoid the ancient practice of trading rounds, a system of reciprocity that fosters "dutiful, ritualistic drinking," according to a sociologist critical of it. If you meet a friend, he'll treat you to a pint, and you're obliged to do the same for him, but if a third party enters the fray, it spells trouble for a two-pint man. Worse still, if your little band of comrades is sufficiently jolly, you'll attract some hangers-on, and that leads to more pints, because the Irish are drawn to sociability like moths to a flame. The writer Benedict Kiely, on holiday in Dublin, once remarked that while he strolled the seventy-five yards from O'Connell Bridge to the White Horse Bar, fourteen people invited him to have a drink.

When it came to the rounds system, I had a nemesis—Moriarity, the photographer, as I'll call him. He seldom drank at Birchall's, preferring the artsy central pubs where young women gather, so I rarely saw him, and though I enjoyed his company, I regretted the times he'd corralled me. Bearded and graying, with a full head of curly hair, Moriarity played the rascal to the hilt, but he was also a brilliant talker on painting, literature, politics, and so on. When we first met, purely by chance, the conversation was so stimulating I finished my third pint before I knew it, and that forced me to ask for another round, after which the demonic Moriarity snuck in a fifth pint—he must have whispered the order, because I didn't hear it—and thereby committed me to a sixth, although I begged off by citing my status as a blow-in who lacked the capacity of certain citizens of the Republic.

Too much sociability can be a killer. As the speed of the rounds escalates, you feel surrounded by an invisible force field. Why won't your feet move? What malign neural malfunction prevents you from leaving? H. L. Mencken's *Dictionary of the American Language* supplies a long list of slang terms for being drunk, but the Irish are no slouches, either. They're spannered, rat-arsed, cabbaged, and hammered; ruined, legless, scorched, and blottoed; or simply trolleyed or sloshed. In Kerry, you're said to be flamin'; in Waterford, you're in the horrors; and in Cavan, you've gone baloobas, a tough one to wrap your tongue around if you *are* baloobas. In Donegal, you're steamin', while the afflicted in Limerick are out of their tree. Those who suffer in Louth have taken a ride on the bingo bus.

Overindulgence of the garden variety is no sin in the eyes of most publicans, though, unless you're sloppy, cause a scene, bug the other customers, are verbally abusive, or pick a fight. (If a man takes off his jacket, he's praying the fight won't happen, says the lore.) Still, a tiny number of people at any pub turn into awful pests. The reasons for their profligacy are legion, but a publican has just one option to counteract it—he must bar the offender, sometimes for life. (The term "eighty-sixed" isn't used in Ireland, but the phrase "on the wagon" has an Irish link. W. A. McIntire, New York's sanitation commissioner, collected drunks with a water wagon in 1910.) I know a publican who has barred hundreds over the past forty years, and he once confided how delicate the process can be.

You can't pounce in the heat of the moment, he told me. Barring is a cagey affair. The guilty party, showing off to a crowd, will be full of bravado, so you have to play a waiting game and sandbag him later when he's alone, vulnerable, and—ideally—hungover. In most cases, he's already been issued a warning, but he'll still grovel, protest, and try to enlist his mates as character witnesses. This is useless, because the mates are afraid they'll be barred, too. The offender's left to dangle. He racks his brain for the perfect excuse to be reinstated and hits on it at last—a family funeral! (The second most common excuse is the desperate need to watch a big football match with the guys.) The mourners will adjourn to the pub after the ceremony, he whines, but the plea falls on deaf ears. Motion denied! Only a half dozen times has my publican friend ever reversed a decision.

Around nine o'clock, Birchall's slides into a mellow middle zone that precedes the calamitous scramble for drinks at last call. Women have filtered into the pub by now, on their own or with a partner, and that was inconceivable as late as the 1960s. Until the Equal Status Act of 2000 made it illegal to discriminate on the basis of sex, many publicans could and did ban women from the premises, or confine them to a snug. (Country matchmakers, operating in a time warp, still use these screened-off private alcoves to broker marriages.) To get around such obstacles, a woman might pass a jug through the door, or send a child to have it filled. During the nineteenth century, they began to frequent spirit grocers, where alcohol, primarily cheap gin, was sold with the tea, butter, and eggs. These "gin palaces," tastefully appointed, with soft gas lighting, were luxurious compared to the dingy, grimy local of the period as captured, once again, by Flann O'Brien, who knew whereof he spoke.

"No Irishman could feel at home in a pub," O'Brien wrote, "unless he was sitting in deep gloom on a hard seat with a very sad expression on his face, listening to the drone of bluebottle squadrons carrying out a raid on the yellow sandwich cheese."

Women are welcome at most pubs these days. Some pubs even court them with plush furnishings. From an economic standpoint, they're a valuable asset, because they tend to ask for wine or spirits, a more expensive proposition than Guinness. If they do order stout, they may opt for a "ladylike" glass, the word for a half pint in Ireland, rather than a full one. At Birchall's, a pint of Guinness costs about $6.30—lager is higher—while a glass costs about $3.75, so the house wins again. An astute publican keeps a tally of such statistics in his or her head, and can put a price tag on every regular. Someone who drinks three pints of stout five nights a week spends about five thousand a year, and that's one reason why the eccentricities of some customers are so readily tolerated.

Over the next few months, I bellied up to the bar at Birchall's and estimated my annual worth at about $1,500, a mere drop in the bucket. Like most regulars, I also became hyperaware of the pub's routine and noticed the slightest change in it. If the stout was a little too cold, or the lights a little too bright, I registered the divergence as sensitively as a seismograph, although not all the changes were so discreet. The most sweeping concerned the bar's staff. When I arrived in Dublin, the city was overwhelmingly white and Irish, but immigrants were pouring into the country from such new EU member states as Poland and Romania, as well as from places like China, India, and Russia, and often they were young, ambitious, and eager for the entry-level jobs at pubs that Ireland's young people usually snub now because they have far better options.

So it was that Birchall's hired a Chinese man and woman, both in their twenties, as floor staff, the rough equivalent of waiters.

They circled during the busy evening hours to deliver drinks, collect the empties, and take the pressure off the frazzled barmen. The woman left abruptly, but Zhang Ning, reinvented as Andy, stayed on, and through his grit and intelligence, he rose to the position of a full-fledged barman with a decent rate of pay. Andy is compact, witty, and totally acculturated, admired for his banter and his cool, dressed in the hippest threads he can afford and capable of a showy haircut, but tourists are sometimes surprised when they see him behind the bar.

An official at the Irish Tourist Board once expressed a slight concern about all the foreigners working in pubs, because when the Kellys from Cleveland travel to Ireland as "roots tourists" to look up their ancestors at the National Library, they expect Seamus O'Halloran to pull their pint—not Andy, who doesn't have red hair, freckles, or any other attribute of the stage Irishman. (This is short-sighted of the official, of course. The Chinese chef at Smyths cooks the best Irish stew in Ranelagh.) As for Andy, he's accustomed to how much the customers drink, a lot by the standards of China, but he doesn't judge and feels grateful for the chance to start a new life. It would be nice if Dublin had a Zhang Ning pub someday, but Andy's content for the moment and so accepted by everybody that he hosts a karaoke night during the Ranelagh Arts Festival every autumn.

If the regulars adapted easily to Andy, they were saddened and a bit unmoored when Jack Birchall chose to retire. "A shock to the system," I heard somebody say. Maybe Jack's intimates knew about his decision, but I only learned of it after the pub was sold. Again, there was no sign posted to tip me off. The deal was private, and among the principals was Frank Smyth of Smyths, who had a partner and presented an offer at just the right time, when Jack was ready to quit and enjoy life. His four grown children, three daughters and a son, had no desire to take over the pub— that's generally the case in publicans' families these days. The children have far better options, too, and prefer to invest their inheritance elsewhere rather than put in long, tedious hours listening to the scintillating opinions of folks like me.

I bumped into Jack not long after the deal had closed. He had a better tan than ever and was about to fly to Biarritz for a two-week summer holiday, and if he missed his bar rag, it didn't show. Frank Smyth was in the thick of it, though, with two pubs to run instead of one. If you watch Frank in action, you'd never figure him as an owner. He works so tirelessly, and at such a brisk pace, you assume he's trying to impress the boss and earn a promotion. Jack made the task look effortless and carried it off with savoir faire, but Frank, who's much younger, hurries and scurries, as if he's late for an important meeting. He's a barman of the professional school, too, and had started with Jack in the Liberties, then spent fourteen years at Birchall's before he opened Smyths in 2000.

As a pro, Frank understood he'd be treading on eggshells with the gang at Birchall's. They'd subject his every move to intense scrutiny. When he displayed some harmless rugby jerseys for a spot of color, one regular accused him of a lapse in taste. The jerseys were "too in your face," he was told. I didn't care about the rugby gear myself, but I was mildly disconcerted about the new toasted sandwiches. Toasties are a staple at most pubs and come in many varieties—cheese, ham-and-cheese, and ham-cheese-tomato-and-onion, the vaunted "special," for example—and though they're exactly what the doctor didn't order, I became addicted to them.

There's no better pub lunch than a toastie and a pint, although you may fall asleep afterward and wake up a fat man, as I nearly did until I kicked the habit.

On Jack's watch, the toasties were prepared from scratch. Jack was a genius at it, really. He layered the ingredients neatly, clamped the sandwich into a mesh grill, and popped it into a toaster. There was never a false move. He never retracted the grill before the cheese had melted, an oversight that occurs more often than you'd like to believe. Next he cut the toastie into quarters, each scorched with lovely grill marks, and sprinkled a garnish of potato chips on the plate, but Frank quite sensibly began to import ready-made toasties from his award-winning kitchen down the block. The sandwiches, wrapped in cellophane, were more hygenic, he said, and so foolproof even the clumsiest barman could heat one in a toaster oven without any fuss.

Still, I missed the old toasties. I missed the grill marks and the potato chips—I missed things as they were and always had been, I suppose, but my distress couldn't compare to the grumbling of some aged veterans when Frank installed a big flat-screen TV on a wall. They called it a "monster," yet Frank argued that it was essential to keep the sports fans happy, or they'd go somewhere else. There were other disagreements, as well. One veteran, incensed about a perceived breach of etiquette, mounted a boycott and led twenty-one of his pals to Corrigan's—a potential loss of one hundred thousand dollars or so, if they were all worth five grand a year. The dispute was finally resolved through negotiation, though, and the ringleader and his crew returned to the stalwart stools and chairs they'd no doubt pined for during their brief rebellion.

The last thing Frank wanted was to offend his core clientele, but nobody in his right mind would deny the fact that the pub needed some work—and not just cosmetic work, although Frank and his partner also had plans to redecorate. There were plenty of minor repairs to be done, he told me once. The toilets were clean, for instance, but outmoded. Some women had complained about it to Frank, and swore they wouldn't be back until he could provide bright, modern facilities. A dodgy back entrance to the pub offered an ideal opportunity for shady characters to wander in, perhaps with an ulterior motive in mind, and that had to be fixed, too, and a new door added, to keep out the riffraff.

Frank's plans hardly sounded drastic or sensational, yet whenever you fiddle with an institution, it wobbles a bit. Nobody knows for sure which pillar or beam supports the mystery, so a wrong move has the power to bring down the whole structure. That would be a tragedy for Birchall's. As a traditional pub, it was a triumph of the familiar and the everyday, and its homey comforts served its customers as an anchor in a rapidly growing city that might otherwise confuse or intimidate them. By its very nature, it suggested a reassuring continuity, and the regulars depended on the illusion that it would stay the same forever. What drew them back, time and again, was something ineffable, along with the craic, of course, and a treasured feeling of friendship and belonging.

Having lived in Dublin for a while, I couldn't claim to be an innocent anymore. I'd been disabused of my naïve conception of Ireland as an enchanted place, where change happens slowly if it happens at all. Indeed, the Irish were devouring change with their breakfast, or being devoured by it—one couldn't say for certain. Change floated over the island like a powdery, transformative dust, and if it settled on your shoulders you, too, might be transformed, although the end result, as with any hastily performed act of magic, couldn't be calculated in advance. Your only choice was to put one foot in front of the other and stride toward a largely positive vision of the future, although you risked leaving the lessons of the past behind.

Such lessons are the blood, bone, and marrow of traditional pubs, but the pubs, too, were changing by the hour—or simply dying off in rural areas, at the alarming rate of one per day. The developers in the city were knocking them down to build apartments and stores, and paying a fortune for the privilege. The Foxhunter in suburban Lucan, blessed with three acres, had recently fetched $20.5 million at auction, for instance. One out of every three pubs sold in County Dublin in 2007 was bought for its land, not its trade, and though Birchall's would be spared that fate, its future was unclear. In the new Ireland of Range Rovers, security alarms, and pistachio oil, was there still room for a quiet place apart devoted solely to talk and drink? That was a question worth investigating.

Chapter 4

THE ANCIENT BIRTHPLACE
OF GOOD TIMES

THOUGH THE PUBLIC house has long been central to Ireland's social life, it has never received the sort of scholarly attention it deserves, I discovered at the National Library, a grand old building in Dublin, where I took up residence in the Reading Room to explore its history. Contrary to popular opinion, the pub isn't even an Irish invention, but they were ready to embrace the idea, having brewed ale for centuries. St. Patrick, the scourge of snakes and sinners, counted a brewer among his entourage—the priest Mescan, who was said to be "without evil"—while St. Brigid made her own beer and once turned a leper's bathwater into a bucket of suds by blessing it, according to the hagiographers. Monasteries provided ale with meals and offered it as sustenance to travelers. One monastery thought it so high in nutrition that the friars were supplied with a gallon a day.

Only when the Normans invaded in the twelfth century did the first taverns appear in Dublin. The Normans were serious lovers of wine, who imported bordeauxs and burgundies from France by ship, sometimes swapping for fish or hides. They also depended on lesser varietals, or *vini corrupti*, from Spain and England, adulterating them with ginger, cinnamon, and other spices to mask the dreadful flavor. Wine was not unknown as a breakfast beverage, nor was the meal a light repast, at least for the prior of Holy Trinity, who enjoyed a few glasses of red with his roast goose or pigeon. At first the shops that cropped up on Winetavern Street sold casks for the domestic use of the nobility—the Normans categorized the Irish as "foreigners"—but gradually people of the professional class met in them to drink and conduct their daily business.

The Normans liked their ale, too, and most households employed a brewer, while in Irish homes the task fell to women, whose ale was sweet and unhopped. (Hops won't grow in Ireland's cool climate.) Some women acquired a reputation for being the best in their local area—hence, the term "local" to denote a pub—and sold what they produced, yet the demand was so constant and wide-reaching that quality was scarcely a concern. "Any woman, if her credit will serve to borrow a pan, and to buy but a measure of malt, setts up brewing," one observer wrote. The "pan" was a brewer's cauldron, and they could be had at any street market. Soon the Irish followed the example of their occupiers and drank their purchases on the spot, a custom that gave birth to the dank, smelly, flea-ridden alehouses of the poor, where mangy dogs wandered among the dreary, sodden customers.

The Norman influence faded over time, hastened by the Black Death, or bubonic plague, that killed off a third to a half of Ireland's population between 1347 and 1351. The displaced Irish also embarked on a series of risings and recaptured their estates, while the Normans themselves began to mimic the habits of the "foreigners" they had oppressed and blended in among the natives. The distinction between a tavern and an alehouse started to blur, and the two ultimately melded and evolved into the public house. Though the food at pubs could be exceptional, with salmon and oysters fresh from the sea, the rooms were often filthy and reprehensible, and gambling and prostitution flourished.

"There are whole streets of taverns," sighed Barnabe Rich, an English soldier who lived in the city, "and it is a rare thing to find a house in Dublin without a tavern, as to find a tavern without a strumpet." The strumpets were so numerous that a decree was passed in 1561 ordering alehouse proprietors to post a sign on their doors stating their intent to "extirpate whoredom." Any woman on the premises was assumed to be for hire, causing one of the accused to respond with a rejoinder clever enough to be recorded for posterity. "I was 'tis true for debt in jail," she protested, "but never got my living by my tail."

Oddly, ale was almost unknown in rural Ireland, where the spirits of choice were whiskey, first introduced in the fifteenth century, and poteen, a bootleg liquor usually distilled from a mash of potatoes, grain, and yeast. On the other hand, Dublin was so awash in ale that the British authorities felt compelled to stem its effects on the army of inebriates who stumbled through the streets, relieving themselves as necessary and sleeping where they collapsed. The first government act to try to curtail the spread of pubs became law in 1635—although its purpose was also political, as the journalist Cian Molloy has pointed out.

Many mishiefes and inconveniences doe arise from the excessive number of alehouses, from the erection of them in woods, bogges, and other unfit places, and many of them not in towne-ships, but dispersedly, in dangerous places, and kept by unknown persons not under-taken for, whereby many times they become receptacles for rebels and other malefactors and harbours of gamesters and other idle, disordered, and unprofitable livers, and that those that keep those alehouses for the most part are not fitted or furnished to lodge or entertaine travelers in any decent manner.

The act failed miserably. By 1667, there were 1,500 licensed premises in Dublin, while one third of the city's residences were serving drinks by 1710, so the "unprofitable livers" failed to be inconvenienced and continued on their merry way. The battle lines were drawn, though, with the forces of order and rectitude on one side and those of Bacchus and chaos on the other. Colonel Richard Lawrence, a Cromwellian planter, belonged to the former camp. He hated drink even more than he despised the pope, and he published a pamphlet in 1682 that showed exactly how much, by his own arithmetic, the "wealth-wasting lusts" of the Irish cost each year.

Swearing, 20,000 pounds
Gambling, 52,000 pounds
Adultery, 67,000 pounds
Drunkenness, 210,000 pounds

Even priests were victims of the booze epidemic. Oliver Plunkett, the Archbishop of Armagh, begged his peers to stay out of pubs and quit bingeing on whiskey. "And since deeds speak louder than words," said Plunkett, in a gesture of supreme self-sacrifice, "I never take a drink between meals. Let us remove this defect from an Irish priest, and he will be a saint."

The Lord's Day Act of 1685 forbade pubs from opening during the hours of divine worship, but again it had little impact on the general revelry. The ability of Dubliners to misbehave had reached epic proportions, as this doggerel about the antics of drunken tradesmen attests:

> Wine they swallow down like fishes
> Now it flies about in glasses
> Now they toast their dirty lasses
> Now they throw away their poses
> Hats and wigs fly all about
> Now they part with heavy curses
> Broken heads and empty purses.

Worse lay ahead when gin, already a blight in London, reached the shores of Ireland in the early eighteenth century. William of Orange, who wanted no truck with the French and had put a stop to any shipments of brandy, was its champion. Cheap and potent, gin spawned an underworld of purgatorial shops where, for just pennies, you could stay drunk for days at a time. At century's end, one quarter of all the deaths in Ireland of adults over twenty could be ascribed to the abuse of alcohol. Poverty was at the core of the problem, of course, along with the hideous living conditions it fostered, but some theorists have suggested that the Irish, as a deprived and colonized people, may have deliberately, if unconsciously, chosen to dull the senses.

Ale remained the preferred tipple in pubs, but the alewife brewers had surrendered the territory to professionals by then. More than ninety breweries were scattered around Dublin, with the densest concentration on James's Street by the Liffey, once part of a "whipping run" where wrongdoers felt the sting of the lash in full public view. If you stroll there from Stephen's Green, you feel as if you're traveling back in time, leaving behind the fancy shops on Grafton Street and skirting Trinity College before you turn toward Christ Church Cathedral and the Liberties, where the sidewalks are crowded with residents, especially women pushing prams, out for a breath of fresh air. On James's Street, you can read the city's age in the cobbled pavement and fortresslike structures, none more somber and invincible looking than the Guinness complex, the only brewery in the area still in business.

The tale of Arthur Guinness, the firm's founder, is so familiar in Ireland that some schoolchildren can probably recite it from memory. Born in Celbridge, County Kildare in 1725, where his father worked as the steward to Archbishop Price of Cashel and brewed the estate's beer, he inherited two hundred pounds sterling on the archbishop's death and invested it in a brewery in nearby Leixlip, also in Kildare, operating it with his brother Richard. Three years later, he moved to Dublin and signed a nine-thousand-year lease on a defunct brewery at St. James's Gate for forty-five pounds per annum—a lease that's still in effect. The three-acre property included draft horses, a hayloft, and plenty of rats.

Though the location was excellent, allowing Guinness to transport kegs down the river on barges, he soon realized how difficult it would be to crack the city's market. The excise laws gave the English a leg up on the Irish, who were also obliged to buy their hops only from colonial suppliers at an inflated price, so beer imported from England cost the publicans much less. Only when "Uncle Arthur" decided to stop brewing ale in 1779 and concentrate on porter did his luck begin to change.

The credit for inventing porter ordinarily goes to Ralph Harwood of the Bell Brewhouse in Shoreditch, who developed it around 1722. Before that, England's bestselling beer was three-thread, possibly a blend of pale ale, new brown ale, and stale brown ale. A publican did the mixing, but Harwood's Entire, a bitter, dark-brown beer, required no fuss and came in a single cask ideal for export. It got its name from the men who "ported" goods at such London markets as Covent Garden and Smithfield. They had adopted the brew as their own, and swallowed it with the gusto of dockers. Guinness's version, officially ruby-colored, was darker, richer, and more full-bodied than the original—a "stouter" porter, later simply stout. Its secret ingredient was a special strain of yeast whose clone is still around, supposedly kept under lock and key in the Directors' Safe at St. James's Gate.

Arthur Guinness, though a kind employer, could not be called politically progressive. When he opposed the Society of United Irishmen, a group dedicated to bridging the religious divide, reforming parliament, and ending England's dominion, his stout was pilloried as "Black Protestant Porter." In fact, the company was slow to hire Catholics and instead put teetotalers at the top of its list, because they were so dependable. Guinness's attitude toward its employees has always been patriarchal, and it isn't unusual for three or four generations of a family to have worked there. Boys in search of a job used to sit for an aptitude test in their early teens, and if they had a relative with the firm, they received a gold star on their exam that granted them preferential treatment. For the most part, they ran errands, but one boy was assigned the task of feeding raw fish to the cats that killed the rats. They got no free stout, of course, but adults did, still two pints a day at stations around the plant into the 1970s.

The plant covers fifty-five acres at St. James's Gate. The Guinness Storehouse, a sort of museum with a plentifully stocked, logo-heavy gift shop, is Ireland's leading tourist attraction, having surpassed the Book of Kells. If you take the self-guided tour, you'll learn that the word "beer" derives from the Anglo-Saxon for barley, a cereal that grows handily in the acidic soil of the Republic. Guinness buys about ninety thousand tons a year, or two thirds of the country's production. Hops come from abroad, with the most desirable found south of the equator. The water isn't drawn from the Liffey, although a few drinkers believe that it is, just as they subscribe to a hoary legend about a brewery worker who once drowned in a vat and lent the stout a remarkably delicious flavor as he decomposed. Streams in the mountains of Kildare are the actual source, and the soft water has a low mineral content, with hints of calcium and magnesium sulfate.

Do you care that Robert Louis Stevenson had some Guinness sent to him when he was living in Samoa? Or that Guinness Foreign Export in bottles, almost twice as strong as keg stout, is considered an aid to sexual potency in Africa and the Caribbean? Maybe, maybe not. But you're sure to be astonished by the sheer thrust of the company's marketing efforts when your tour concludes at the glass-fronted Gravity Bar, seven floors above the city. The bar, closed to the ordinary public, gives you a magnificent

360-degree view, and while you savor your single complimentary pint—you can't buy a second, so don't bother to try—you'll marvel at how the firm has made James Joyce part of the team by stenciling quotes from his books on the windows, just as it features a harp, the national symbol, on its glassware and cans. Guinness *is* Ireland, the branding suggests, and it forges a bond so absolute that you'll feel unpatriotic if you don't finish your jar.

The presence of Guinness may be inescapable in Dublin, but the Irish taste for it has been declining sharply for the past few years, with pub sales down by 7 percent in 2007. (A new ad campaign launched in 2008 has increased the turnover at off-licenses, though.) To address the trend toward lager, the company has tested a series of lighter occasional brews such as North Star, and also Guinness "lite" at 2.7 percent alcohol, but the beers died a slow death at Birchall's and elsewhere. In some quarters, stout is regarded as an old man's drink, good for reveries but too heavy and torpor-inducing to yield the instant buzz young clubbers crave—they can knock back a pint of Carlsberg much faster. Solitary contemplatives such as Tom Corkery may be as antique as thatched roofs someday, but the future of the Guinness brand is global, anyway, with about two thirds of the business already done abroad.

The global push began shortly after Guinness merged with Grand Metropolitan, a food-industry giant (Burger King, Pillsbury, Häagen-Dazs, Alpo Petfoods) in 1997 to form Diageo, the world's leading distributor of premium drinks (Smirnoff, Johnnie Walker, Tanqueray, Jose Cuervo, and others). Diageo brews Irish Budweiser at the St. Francis Abbey in Kilkenny, but its ambitions are far more extensive and stretch across 180 countries and territories. The black stuff is brewed in about fifty of them, including Nigeria, the brand's second-largest consumer behind Britain. (Ireland lags in third place.) Nigerian sales rose by 18 percent in 2007, sparked by TV ads that praise Guinness as the "home of greatness," whatever that means. Moreover, Diageo does its best to promote the notion that an "Irish" pub will be a lucrative investment anywhere on earth, thereby increasing the number of outlets for its stout and other beers and whiskeys.

One wants to doubt such boldness, but it happens to be true. Diageo-Guinness USA, a division of Guinness Limited, spreads the gospel through the Irish Pub Concept, initiated in Germany in 1992 to "facilitate the development of authentic, high quality Irish pubs outside Ireland." Among its recruiting tools is a Web site, whose claims could not be called modest. Investors who adhere to the IPC model achieve a success rate of 99 percent, the site all but guarantees, since they get the benefits of a branded franchise without any of the royalties, fees, or rules. The IPC focuses on four key elements that make an "Irish" pub special, even if it's in Toledo— the design and ambience; a friendly bar staff with some real Irish members; Irish music, live or recorded, and entertainment; and Irish food and drink. DGUSA helps an investor pull together the package through advice, referrals, and training sessions.

For would-be publicans, DGUSA provides tips on real estate and location, as well as introductions to potential sources of capital. It sells the Irish Pub Concept Business Plan ($500) and the apparently less informative Insider's Guide to the Irish Pub Concept ($50). It directs clients to an agency that can supply Irish staffers, who have the proper visas and an ability to combine "humor and hospitality," and to dealers in Irish and Guinness-branded bric-a-brac. Also available are copies of the Irish Pub Food Recipe

Book, although it costs $150 if purchased outside the training course. The sound system of choice is DMX's Profusion X, a device that adapts its music to the time of day and the customers' energy level. Buyers are instructed in "How to Pour the Perfect Pint," too, a line that actually bears a Guinness trademark and sets a new standard for corporate overkill that the folks at Coca-Cola would envy.

For the all-important design & build phase, the IPC Web site has links to several approved, independently owned firms. The Irish Pub Company in Dublin is among the oldest and most visible, and perhaps the most active and profitable, so I arranged to meet with Noel Darby, a company rep, to hear more about it. It's the brainchild of Mel McNally, Darby explained over coffee. He described McNally as an architect and a potter, who has a solid head for business. McNally founded the company in 1991 to foster his dream of turning the Irish pub into a marketable commodity, much as Guinness was doing at the same time, so he took a year off to travel and study the subject in detail, researching the origins and history of pubs until he devised five distinctive prototypes—Country Cottage, Brewery, Gaelic, Victorian Dublin, and, yes, Traditional.

To date, the Irish Pub Company has built about five hundred pubs in forty-five countries. Italy, its foremost client, has almost reached the saturation point, with more than a hundred Harrington & Son–style operations strung from Milan to Palermo. (Names must be chosen carefully, the Irish Pub Concept site suggests. The tag "& Son" confers a patina of history.) There's no shortage of new applicants, though, with plenty of prospective moguls in Russia, China, and Dubai, where the company already has twenty employees, clamoring for an opportunity. Some projects are small and simple, Darby noted, while others are huge and complex, such as Nine Fine Irishmen, the pub McNally and his crew cooked up for MGM's New York-New York Hotel & Casino on the Vegas strip. The Irishmen led a futile rising in 1848, but that hasn't hurt business. With its slogan "A place for stout hearts, powerful convictions, and strong livers," the pub has been a huge hit and grosses about $14 million a year.

McNally not only dreams, designs, and throws pots—he, too, invests in pubs. He and a partner own the Fadó chain, the biggest in America with fourteen branches, and also Guinness's thirstiest U.S. customer. You can't lose with an "Irish" pub—that was Noel Darby's message, an echo of DGUSA's, and he pulled out some data to back it up. If a British pub switches to an Irish theme, say, and refits its interior with tin signs, etched Jameson mirrors, and so on, its profits frequently triple. The average monthly turnover at an Irish pub is nearly four times greater than at an American bar of the same size. A pub—Country Cottage or otherwise—can be designed and built in about eighteen weeks, and it should pay for itself in twelve to eighteen months, Darby promised, with thirty-six months as an outside figure.

"I've never known a pub to fail," he claimed, so gratified investors often snap up a second and then a third. Pierre Doyle began with an O'Reilly's in Amsterdam in 1994, for instance, and has since sprinkled around O'Reilly's in Dublin, Heidelberg, and Brussels. A prime location is essential, Darby allowed, as is good management, but the single factor that matters most is the "authenticity of replication." That gave me pause. The authenticity I fell for at McSorley's (& Sons!) proved to be phony, and it would be doubly so if you copied it and transplanted it elsewhere—in Guam, say—but most people don't seem to care. As long as they can imagine they're in Ireland, the natives of Guam—and the Italians, the Spaniards, the Americans, and so forth—are able to ignore the fact that they've never left home at all.

By accident, I later came across a paper at the National Library that advanced a theory to account for this curious syndrome. Published in the *Journal of Consumer Research* under the incredibly verbose title "Consumer Perception of Iconicity and Indexicality and Their Influence on Assessments of Authentic Market Offerings," its authors asserted that most scholars "agree that authenticity is not an attribute inherent in an object, and is better understood as an assessment made by a particular evaluation in a particular context." In other words, authenticity is in the eye of the beholder, a conclusion I found difficult to accept. Maybe Ireland truly is the Ancient Birthplace of Good Times, though, where "it's like being in a nineteenth century novel, with better food and a happier ending," as the Irish Tourist Board had put it in a recent promotion.

One Saturday afternoon, I took a break from my diligent research and dashed through the rain that fell all that June, once again quashing my dream of a sweltering Irish summer, to Paddy Power, a bookmaker on Lower Baggot Street, where I placed a bet on the Ascot Gold Cup, the race James Joyce commemorated before he went to work for Guinness. It would have been far too simple to indulge my literary side and settle on Yeats, the favorite and eventual winner, so I threw my money at Sergeant Cecil instead, and when he refused to march toward victory, I consoled myself at Doheny & Nesbitt, conveniently located right across the way.

Nesbitt's, as it's known, is a trophy. The Irish Pub Company might call the look Victorian Dublin, but only the front bar, with its snugs, mirrored partitions, and ornate ceiling of papier mâché, is original, while the back bar or lounge is just authentically replicated. It draws a mixed crowd of professionals who take a serious interest in sports, so I expected the place to be jam-packed with gamblers like Nosey Flynn, doomed to search eternally through the pages of *Ulysses* for a hot tip he never gets, but Nesbitt's was deserted except for an Italian tourist, who sat reading *Corriere della Serra* rather than the *Racing Post*. In the echoing vacancy, I thought I heard another sigh escape from the lips of tradition.

I drank a pint, anyway, and tried to parse the reasons for the success of the "Irish" pub as a commodity for export. What was the secret? DGUSA had even introduced a new wrinkle with its portable, free-standing pub (thirty-six kegs sold at JFK Airport in the first month!) and the Irish Snug Pub, a close cousin (eighty kegs at Fenway Park on the first weekend!). Mel McNally's group offered some possible explanations—the craic, the ambience, the casual sociability, the chance for people to relax and be themselves—but I still sensed other factors at work, although I couldn't put my finger on them, not yet.

Ireland's woeful battle with alcohol worsened during the nineteenth century, I learned on my return to the library. Whiskey, once a luxury of the elite, had filtered down to street level and spawned a legion of dram shops, where you could buy "a poison productive of vice, riot, and disease, hostile to all habits of decency, honesty, and industry, and, in short, destructive to the souls and bodies of our fellow creatures," as the Reverend James Whitelaw harangued in 1805. Yet the British House of Commons, looking into the issue a few years later, wondered if whiskey might not be indispensable to the Irish as a palliative against the cold, damp weather. Its medicinal uses were manifold, in fact. When combined with boiled nettles, it was prescribed as a cure for measles.

The devotees of whiskey were immune to such chastisement, naturally, and would have agreed instead with the analysis of Richard Stanihurst, a contributor to Holished's *Chronicles*, who once sang the praises of malt. A dram had the power to keep "the head from whirling, the eies from dazeling, the toong from lisping, the mouth from maffling, the teeth from chattering," and so on, Stanihurst wrote, although he added a caveat, "if it be orderly taken." That warning, too, was roundly ignored. Whiskey and every other drink were "taken" in corrosive measures. One trick of the gentry, who kept elaborate cellars, was to serve wine in a stemless glass that forced the guests to gulp it down before it spilled and lose their bearings sooner rather than later. When young blades met to carouse, they might ask the tavern boy to remove their shoes, hide them, and scatter broken glass by the door to keep anyone from leaving early.

Though drunkards might be a public embarrassment, casting the Irish in a negative light and shoring up a stereotype, the truth was more complicated. A great many citizens of the Republic never touched a drop. Almost all women abstained, as did the devoutly religious, both Catholic and Protestant, and the abstainers often joined church-led temperance crusades that were largely ineffectual until Father Theobald Mathew, a charismatic Capuchin dedicated to helping the poor, assumed control of the Cork Total Abstinence Society in 1838. The impact of the

"Apostle of Temperance" was immediate. In less than a year, the society's membership jumped from a few dozen people to about 130,000 in Cork alone. Between November and December 1839, Father Mathew signed up about 230,000 members in Limerick and Waterford. By 1843, about half of Ireland's adult population had taken the pledge to forgo alcohol in all its murderous forms, and that led to a significant reduction in crime. The drunkards had even vanished in some towns.

"On visiting the public houses of my own district during the night," wrote the astonished A. B. Hill, a constable in Dunmore, County Kilkenny, "I found them closed and the inmates in bed, a stranger proof of the working of the Society I could not adduce."

The pledge itself was simple. "I promise to abstain from all intoxicating drinks, except used medicinally, and by the order of a medical man," it went, "and to discountenance the cause and practice of intemperance." (The medical proviso was dropped later.) Those willing to recite it, usually poor and illiterate, were rewarded with pamphlets, a numbered pledge card, and a medal. On one side, the medal showed a happy family sitting by the fire. The husband held a banner that read "Prosperity," while his wife's banner celebrated "Domestic Comfort." Swans and doves cavorted to convey the benefits of an idyllic alcohol-free existence, but the medal's other side portrayed the evils of Demon Whiskey. A frothing drunk was about to bean his wife in the head with a hammer, cheered on by an audience of serpents and vultures.

In Dublin, Father Mathew's crusade stumbled. When he reached the city in 1840, the big crowds did not materialize, and the press treated him more harshly than it did in the provinces. Still, the society continued to exert a substantial degree of control, and its grip over the committed was very nearly absolute until it began to unravel. Some believe the church let the apostle down by not lending him its unqualified support, but his inability to enlist Ireland's middle and upper classes also hurt the movement. Father Mathew's finances were a shambles, as well. He required three secretaries to answer his mail, ran up a large printing bill for his pamphlets, and was a soft touch who gave too generously to marching bands and other temperance affiliates. In 1844, he endured the humiliation of being arrested for his debts, and his crusade was at an end.

The temptation to backslide was constant for members, of course, and more acute than ever after an increase in whiskey production made the price of a dram even cheaper. Workers were often paid in pubs and encouraged to have at least one drink before they left, and though a man might have taken the pledge and stuck to it in the past, he must have felt his willpower caving in as he labored in the shadow of the Great Famine—during which, surprisingly, there was still plenty of drink around and more than enough bars to serve it. Not until Frederick Shaw, Dublin's recorder in the mid-1850s, clamped down on the number of licenses he granted did the accelerated growth rate of pubs slow down. As a consequence, the value of an average pub jumped by about 500 percent over the next twenty years, and some publicans joined the ranks of the bourgeoisie, dabbled in politics, and became respected pillars of the community.

The cutback in licenses did not affect the city's hard-core crew of drunkards, though. Throughout the 1870s, Dublin outpaced London, ten times its size, when it came to citations for being drunk in public, with one woman racking up 264 convictions in a single year. After the pubs closed, the crew retreated into she-beens (from the Irish *sibin*, alternately "little mug," "weak beer," or "illicit alehouse"), frequently no more than a cramped hovel advertised only by a candle or a hunk of lighted turf in a window. To keep the cops at bay, scouts stood outside and sounded an alarm. The extraordinary craving for alcohol reached its apex, perhaps, with the Whiskey Fire of 1875, when a warehouse in the Liberties burned down and spilled hot whiskey into the street, prompting people to lap it up from the gutter.

Yet some authorities understood that the desire for oblivion was due in part to the wretchedness of tenement life. Early in the twentieth century, almost one third of all Dubliners were confined to scruffy apartment blocks that had no toilets or running water. In general, a family shared one room only, even though most couples had between six and twelve children and sometimes as many as twenty. There might be a bed or two, but children usually slept on straw mattresses on the floor. Cooking was done over an open fire, and the same fire was used to heat up the bathwater. Slop buckets stored in corners or in the hall had to be emptied daily. No one had an ounce of privacy, either, so the pub afforded men, at least, the chance to gather in a more amenable space.

"The workman is blamed for visiting the public house, but it is to him what the club is to the rich man," noted Sir Charles Cameron, chief health inspector of Dublin. "His home is rarely comfortable and in the winter the bright light, the warm fire, and the gaiety of the public house are difficult to resist."

It was inevitable, however, given the scale of the abuse, that a cry for temperance would rise again, this time led by Father James Cullen, a Jesuit, who formed the Pioneer Total Abstinence Association of the Sacred Heart in 1898. At first he accepted only women as members, because he felt they were more spiritual and had witnessed the debilitating effect of liquor on their male cohorts, but he soon changed his mind. Cullen did not crusade in the manner of Father Mathew. Instead, he taught by example. Pioneers wore a pin with an image of the Sacred Heart, and for years potential brides viewed this as a positive sign when they were choosing a husband. Cullen criticized "weary wobblers"—those who drank on the continent, say, but not at home, or who drank only on ceremonial occasions—and endorsed the singing of temperance songs such as the one that recounted the horrors visited on a downtrodden family "after Mary took her drop":

> The children are neglected and our house is poor and bare
> Our parlour once so pretty, scarce a table has or chair
> Our Nell is so neglected that her head is like a mop
> There is no-one now to care her, since Mary took her drop.

Other popular tunes were "Bacchus Dethroned," "Make War on Demon Drink," and "The Sweet Lemonade."

Cullen's message carried tremendous clout among Catholics, who'd been instructed that getting drunk on purpose was a sin, although they found it an easy sin to forgive. As Jack Boyle said of another character in *Juno and the Paycock*, "I don't believe he was ever drunk in his life—sure he's not like a Christian at all." Mild jokes at the clergy's expense also had some currency.

> "Pat," warned the priest, "you are at it again. You must keep away from drink. It is your mortal enemy."

"Wisha, Father," Pat replied. "Wasn't it only Sunday last your Reverence told us to love our enemies?"

"Well, then, if I did," the priest said, "I never told you to swallow them."

The most prominent temperance hero during Cullen's reign was the redoubtable Matt Talbot (1856–1925), a typical child of the tenements, deprived and unable to read, with a hard-drinking disciplinarian of a father and a mother who provided shelter from the storm. At the age of twelve, Talbot went to work for Burke's Wine Merchants in Dublin, dipped into the porter, and often returned home drunk, a habit that multiplied when his father, who was in charge of the bonded liquor at the Custom House, secured a job for him there in order to keep an eye on him. That put Talbot too close to the whiskey, though, and soon he was a debilitated alcoholic and spent the next twelve years in a hazy stupor, squandering his money in pubs until he took the pledge.

Thereafter he lived as rigorously as a stylite in a small room his mother sometimes shared. He slept on rough wooden planks on an iron bed, with a chunk of wood for a pillow, and knelt to eat his meals of stale bread and tea or cocoa, although he liked a little meat as a treat on Christmas Day. When he went to bed, he clutched a statue of the Virgin and Child to his chest and slept for just three and a half hours, then woke to kneel and pray again before he attended early Mass. Under his clothes, he wrapped heavy chains around his body as a form of penance, but no one knew about it until he was rushed to a hospital after a heart attack. Declared the Venerable Matt Talbot in 1973, he cannot be beatified without the proof of a physical miracle. His canonization would require a second, and some would say that's asking a lot.

Meanwhile, Cullen's ministry tightened its hold on the country's abstainers. Yielding to Éamon De Valera's clarion call, "Ireland sober, Ireland free," the troops fighting in World War I occasionally wore the pin, but it also happened that a few of their wives, left in the lurch, drank more heavily in their absence. To emphasize the dangers of overindulgence on women, Cullen once drew a cold-hearted portrait of a drunkard's baby, almost certainly the victim of fetal alcohol syndrome. "When born it is puny, fretful, possibly feeble-minded or an idiot," he said, "and fortunately very often goes to swell the infant mortality rate."

For all the inveighing against the horrors of drink, the culture of pubs still thrived, and that baffled such reformers as George William Russell, or Æ, who complained in 1925 that the Irish had twice as many licensed premises as England and three times as many as Scotland. "Ballyhaunis, with a total population of a thousand, has a drink shop for every twenty of its inhabitants . . . How many of these towns can boast a bookshop, a gymnasium, a public swimming bath or a village hall? Throughout the greater part of rural Ireland such things are still looked on as ridiculous luxuries, and the mark of social progress is demonstrated by the opening of two public houses when one would suffice."

Indeed, most country towns had many more pubs per person than Dublin, and they were often the lair of lonely, bibulous bachelor farmers. In essence, it has been argued, the farmers hit the booze so hard both to relieve their sexual tension and as a substitute for any satisfactory emotional relationships. Patrick Kavanagh painted a devastating picture of one such bachelor in his epic poem "The Great Hunger," which caused a furor in its day with its graphic descriptions and its allusion to masturbation.

> O he loved his mother
> Above all others.
> O he loved his ploughs
> And he loved his cows
> And his happiest dream
> Was to clean his arse
> With perennial grass
> On the bank of some summer stream;
> To smoke his pipe
> In a sheltered gripe
> In the middle of July—
> His face in a mist
> And two stones in his fist
> And an impotent worm on his thigh.

In a curious reversal of roles, some bachelor groups frowned on abstainers and accused them of being morally suspect. Because they didn't drink, the theory went, they couldn't be trusted. An abstainer must be up to something, the farmers believed, and it probably took the shape of cruising for young girls, getting them pregnant, and undermining their character. Yet it was actually the bachelors who ran into trouble when they lost their inhibitions after several jars and a dram or two, consorted with the village prostitute, and contracted venereal diseases.

The Pioneers peaked after World War II. Their Golden Jubilee celebration, held at Croke Park, the national stadium of the

Gaelic Athletic Association in Dublin, attracted ninety thousand supporters in 1949, and throughout the 1950s the organization retained about a half million members around the world. As late as 1968, about half of Ireland's adults claimed to be teetotalers, but the pendulum soon began to swing the other way, so that by 2000 only 13 percent of the population, mostly elderly women, wore the pin. There are still lots of church-affiliated societies for abstainers, though, and the abundance of licensed premises remains a controversial issue, but it's an irrefutable fact that 85 percent of the Irish stop by a pub at least once a month, although not necessarily one that's vested in tradition.

Chapter 5

MIRTH IS GOD'S MEDICINE

WHEN I FINISHED my stint at the National Library, feeling well informed but also slightly daunted, aware of some obstacles I hadn't known about before—manufactured nostalgia, the so-called authenticity of replication—I decided to check out the Brazen Head on Lower Bridge Street, advertised as the country's oldest pub and possibly, if I got lucky, exactly the sort of unspoiled traditional spot I was seeking. My hopes were high due to Edna O'Brien, who portrayed its unaffected nature in *Mother Ireland*. "Behind the counter the proprietess sat drinking tea," she wrote. "The place was full of old furniture, old chairs stacked on top of other chairs, a sideboard, lots of sacking, things. On the tiers of glass shelving were the usual drink bottles, the usual empty bottles, and a candelabra of artificial dust-thick flowers."

The artificial dust-thick flowers sounded good, but what if they were fake, part of a contrived environment such as the Irish Pub Company might create? I'd have to be on my toes. Even the Brazen Head's claim to antiquity—established in 1198, says the sign outside—was disputed in some circles. As Andrew O'Gorman has pointed out, the pub received a license to trade from Charles II in 1668 and may have served travelers before then as a coaching inn, but the current building apparently dates from 1700–1710 and used to be a hotel. Moreover, the owners of Grace Neill's in Donaghadee, County Down, swear their pub is older, since it opened as the King's Arms in 1611. Grace Neill, a former landlady, enjoyed her last drink at the bar in 1918 at the age of ninety-eight, and the place was renamed in her honor. Rumor has it that her ghost, judged to be benign, still haunts the premises.

The Brazen Head does look medieval rather than Georgian, with its stone walls, battlements, and a cobbled courtyard for horses and carriages. It's located in an ancient quarter of Dublin, too, near Christ Church Cathedral, founded by the Viking Sitric Silkbeard about 1028, and a half block from the Liffey, gray-green that afternoon and smelling of the sea. There's a plaque outside that features, yet again, a likeness of James Joyce. It attests to the quality of the food—an award of some kind that casts Joyce, often penniless and hungry in his youth, as a gourmet authority, although he'd probably be more interested in a drink. When he finally came into some money in Paris after the success of *Ulysses*, he preferred white wine to red, "electricity" to "beefsteak." His maternal grandfather ran the Eagle House, a pub in Terenure, so it's no accident *Finnegans Wake* involves the dream life of a Chapelizod publican.

A Polish couple paused to stare at Joyce, read the bold black sign—IRELAND'S OLDEST PUB, EST. 1198—and walked right in. Four women from Spain followed in their wake. They ducked into the courtyard, snapped some photos, and scurried away without so much as a sip of Guinness. The courtyard was a pleasant, open-air space, with ivy-covered walls and lanterns to be lit in the evening, where more tourists were enjoying a late lunch. The pub proper consisted of three rooms with very low ceilings and prominent beams, but there was no trace of O'Brien's proprietress or artificial flowers. The rooms were fairly dark, cozy, and creaky with age, done up with historical photos and posters and a grandfather clock, but I also noticed an assortment of kitsch I hadn't encountered anywhere else in Ireland.

Tacked up behind one bar were some cloth badges from the Marblehead, Massachusetts, and Nutley, New Jersey, fire departments, the U.S. Border Patrol, and the California State University Police, among others. (Why grown men pack such badges to distribute on their trips abroad would be an intriguing topic for a post-doctoral dissertation.) Another wall was covered with inscribed dollar bills—"Wayne State Law, Paul and Chad," "Go Buckeyes, Doug, Michael, and Ed," ad infinitum. Presumably, the Brazen Head had become a magnet for American cops, firemen, and frat boys on the loose, and though I have no bias against any of those parties and had in fact been a wayward frat boy myself, their presence in such numbers, when added to the tourists I'd already observed, raised a question about just how genuine the pub could be.

Until recently, a barman told me, you could rent one of the eight hotel rooms upstairs—no timber framing, just bricks-and-mortar—each with a fireplace and often reserved for lodgers. An English friend of mine had lodged there for a while after he graduated from Trinity, hoping to live cheaply and produce a novel, but he never wrote a word in five years because the bar down below kept seducing him away from his desk. In those days, you could ask for a drink from the hangman's cup, a signal that you were familiar with the Phoenix Park murders and how the Invincibles, a Fenian splinter group, had assassinated Lord Cavendish and his undersecretary in 1882. Surgical knives were the weapons of choice. The hangman of the not-so-invincibles had been a regular at the Brazen Head.

One reason tourists flock to the pub, the barman continued, is the free nightly session of traditional music. I was a trifle suspicious, since authentic traditional sessions tend to be loosely assembled and spontaneous, and they gather momentum in the same way that the randomly distributed craic does. They start slowly and build toward a crescendo instead of adhering to a program set in advance. When I was still an innocent, I once fell into the trap of believing I was listening to the real thing at the Oliver St. John Gogarty in Temple Bar, the city's liveliest, booziest, and most touristy district. Along with being the model for Buck Mulligan, Gogarty, who grew rich as a nose-and-throat surgeon, was an aviator, a senator, and the owner of Ireland's first Rolls-Royce. Inside the pub, a bronze statue of the good doctor, also a poet and bon vivant, presides over the festivities.

If traditional music in Ireland has a patron saint, though, it must be the extraordinary Francis O'Neill, born in West Cork in 1848. The son of a wealthy farmer, O'Neill played the flute and was so good at Greek, Latin, and math that his classmates called him "the professor." He ran away from home at sixteen, off to Cork city with a pound in his pocket, but he couldn't find a job and shipped out to England instead, later traveling through the Mediterranean, the Dardanelles, the Bosporus, and the Black Sea before his twenty-first birthday. In Boston, he signed on with the *Minnehaha*, a full-rigged ship, for a seven-month voyage to Japan, but he was marooned by a shipwreck on the journey home. He managed to scrape by on Baker Island in the South Pacific, living like Crusoe until he and his mates were rescued by the *Zoe*, a brig whose captain supervised a Polynesian crew.

The *Zoe* was short on provisions, so the men subsisted on tea and biscuits and reached Honolulu terribly malnourished—except for O'Neill, who had played an Irish air on a borrowed flute and charmed the Polynesians. They rewarded him with rations of their poi and canned salmon. He was so healthy on arrival that he went directly to California instead of into the hospital, and tried his hand as a shepherd in the Sierra Nevada, only to succumb to the doldrums and ship out again. He taught school in Missouri for a year after that, then moved to Chicago and sailed the Great Lakes until they iced over in winter. He married another Irish émigré there, joined the police force in 1873, and was shot by a notorious burglar a month later. The bullet lodged too close to his spine to be extracted, so he took it with him to his grave—sixty-two years later.

Mishaps aside, Chicago was a fine place for any Irishman to wind up. The city was about 13 percent Irish, with all thirty-two counties represented, including a large contingent from Cork, many of whom had been employed to dig the Illinois and Michigan canals, and they'd brought their love of traditional music to the New World. O'Neill climbed the ladder swiftly and served as chief superintendent of police from 1901 to 1905, but his duties as president of the Chicago Irish Music Club were more significant in the long run. He'd met a host of countrymen on the force, who were experts on such instruments as the fiddle, the flute, the tin whistle, and the uillean pipes, and they'd committed a huge store of tunes to memory.

From "Big Pat" Mahoney, a patrolman from Clare, he learned some rare double jigs and hornpipes, for instance, and he wasn't above recruiting talented musicians to walk a beat, as he did with James O'Neill, a former ironworker, whose command of Ulster favorites was unrivaled. Chief O'Neill couldn't transcribe any music himself, so he relied on James as his arranger, and together they collected the more than eighteen hundred melodies that went into *The Music of Ireland*, published in 1903 and still a definitive resource for musicians, almost biblical in stature, that's known affectionately as "The Book." The Chief even invested in an Edison cylinder phonograph and made some of the earliest field recordings of Irish music ever done.

The Book, a monumental effort, listed 625 airs; 75 Carolans (after Turlough Carolan, the harper and composer, who was blind from smallpox and so beloved that his wake lasted four days and drew more than a thousand mourners); 415 double jigs; 60 slip jigs; 380 reels; 25 hornpipes; 25 long dances; 50 marches; and so on. O'Neill's fieldwork paid tribute to the immense variety of traditional music, a remarkable achievement because the tune is never the same twice. The players improvise, so the tune changes from musician to musician, as it does from region to region. George Petrie, another collector, rarely got two identical settings of an unpublished air. In some instances, Petrie recorded fifty notations of a single melody.

The Irish gift for music can be traced back through time. Indeed, it was among the sole virtues of the natives that Giraldo de Barri, a Norman priest from Wales, admired when he visited the island in 1183. Otherwise he expressed dismay over the sloth and odd behavior of the "barbaric" clan. "I find among these people commendable diligence only on musical instruments, on which they are incomparably more skilled than any nation I have seen," de Barri wrote. "Their style is not . . . deliberate and solemn but quick and lively; nevertheless the sound is smooth and pleasant." He goes on to laud the subtle rhythmic motifs and profusely intricate polyphony, and also the sensuous way the harpers caress their strings.

In his *Irish Minstrels and Musicians*, a companion piece to The Book, Chief O'Neill wrote, "Mirth is God's medicine, and never was there an agency better qualified to administer it than the favorite of the muses." That's how I felt at the Oliver St. John Gogarty when the musicians, seated before a bank of microphones at a table by the door, started their gig. They were four gents of staunch middle age, who were equipped with a flute, a tin whistle, a bodhran, and a guitar. The guitar is a contemporary touch, and some classicists frown on it, although the bodhran, a shallow one-sided drum introduced in the 1960s, is a more recent addition. (The drummer wore a motorcycle T-shirt that said "Orange County Choppers," as if to underscore the fact.) Bodhrans are often made with goat skin, but calf is used on occasion and also, if you heed the gossip, illegal greyhound. The word itself means "deafener."

You rap the bodhran with a two-headed stick, or the palm of a hand. It looks simple, but it isn't if you want to capture any subtlety. The mastery of any traditional instrument comes very slowly and with great patience, because there's so much to be learned and appropriated from other players. Folklore has it that it takes seven years of practice and seven of playing to make a piper. (The uillean pipes evolved from the ancient Irish war pipes early in the eighteenth century.) Sean Ennis, a renowned piper, has remarked that even after twenty-one years, he felt like a beginner. The flute also presents a new set of vagaries to the uninitiated, because the keys are seldom fingered. It's the feathery breath that counts.

The group at Gogarty's didn't engage in patter. They just leaped in and ran through each tune two or three times, although in the old days they might have done six, eight, or ten repetitions. The guitar sounded wrong to my ear, disjunctive against the flute and the bodhran, and the group's air of weary professionalism, along with the mikes and the stack of CDs for sale, robbed the performance of any spontaneity, but the music still had a curious effect on me. Though I was undeniably in Ireland, I imagined that I *wasn't*, only longing for it as Finian had longed for his mythical Glocca Morra in *Finian's Rainbow*. This strange delusion put me into a sort of trance, and I wasn't alone. I could see a dreamy look of yearning on the faces around me, too, some with their eyes closed, all of us lost in a mutually reinforced fantasy.

In retrospect, it's easy to see what had happened. The entire experience had been carefully staged and choreographed—worked over, refined, and tested on countless audiences before. Every critical element of the Irish Pub Concept's formula for success was invoked, whether by accident or not, and when you coupled it to a longing for the changeless, enchanted land I still half-believed in at the time—call it Fairytale Ireland—you had a potent combination. True, no real Dubliner would fall for it, but that was beside the point. Gogarty's wasn't for Dubliners. Here was the pub as theater, as entertainment, but also as caricature—sanitized and packaged—and though the fun it generated was harmless, it amounted to another form of replication.

Traditional music, it's been said, connects the past to the present and closes a circle, and that's the source of its powerful hold on an audience. Even the group at Gogarty's, who were far from pure and might better be described as folk musicians, could tap into the slipstream and squeeze out a little juice. There's a magic to it, as Chief O'Neill demonstrated with the tale of Tullogh McSweeney, a dour piper from Donegal. Poor McSweeney had "no music in him" until he braved a trip to a hilltop fort, confronted the King of the Fairies, and dared him to swap tunes. The king blew him away, piping so brilliantly that dozens of leprechauns in red shoes began to dance. The spectacle drove overwrought McSweeney to his bed, but he recovered and had the music in his grasp forever after.

My trance ended when the guitar player sang a song in English. It broke the group dynamic and shattered the mellow atmosphere, and I returned from Glocca Morra with a thud and woke up to where I actually was, in a pub full of tourists who were pounding down beer and shots of Irish whiskey. As an epicure travels to France for the food, a small percentage of Ireland's visitors come for the drink, and they thrive on the anonymity and behave as they never would at home. Temple Bar is where they choose to do their acting-out, hopping from one pub to the next along Fleet Street from the Auld Dubliner to Fitzsimmons ("4 floors, 4 bars, & 4 DJs—All 4 U") until they're spannered, rat-arsed, cabbaged, and so on.

Like misery, insobriety loves company, so the tourist drunk is never alone in Temple Bar, but the scene after midnight, with its shoving matches, broken bottles, and pools of vomit, isn't for everyone. What all this amounts to, really, is a weird perversion of the measured, convivial imbibing that goes on at a pub such as Birchall's. In *Hair of the Dog*, Richard Stivers's study of Irish drinking and its Irish-American counterpart, the author notes that the drunkard in Ireland is a figure to be pitied, someone who's fallen from grace for any number of reasons but still deserves compassion. "Drink is the good man's weakness," as the proverb has it, but this approach undergoes an odd transformation abroad, in America and elsewhere, and the inebriate becomes the "happy drunk" of stage and screen, a stereotype the Irish find offensive.

If drink is truly the good man's weakness, McDaids on Harry Street must have been a paragon of virtue during its heyday in the postwar 1940s as the pub of choice for Dublin's self-destructive literary stars. I stopped there one afternoon on my way to the Traditional Music Archive, where I planned to bone up before attending a session at the Brazen Head. The writer Anthony Cronin has called the ambience "church-like or tomb-like, according to mood," and I felt a quiet sense of ceremony, along with a flutter of ghosts, as I nursed a pint in the clerestory light flowing through four arched windows of stained glass. On the walls were portraits of Sean O'Casey, Brendan Behan, Patrick Kavanagh, and Joyce, naturally, but none of

Brian O'Nolan, who once insulted the barmen by dipping a pocket hydrometer into his whiskey to be sure it hadn't been diluted.

In the guise of Flann O'Brien, O'Nolan achieved a modest fame around Dublin with *At Swim-Two-Birds*, his first novel, but it only sold about 250 copies in its first edition, a fact he bemoaned. (Graham Greene said it resembled *Tristam Shandy* composed by a fan of Groucho Marx.) A few years after its publication in 1939, he started writing "Cruiskeen Lawn," or "the little brimming jug," for the *Irish Times*, a column that could be witty, sarcastic, sardonic, and nonsensical by turns. "It cannot be too often repeated that I am not for sale," he wrote, in a representative sample. "I was bought in 1921 and the transaction was final and conclusive." Early in his career, he knocked out the column in batches on Sundays and enlisted a pal to do the typing if he was too tipsy, then made the round of pubs during the week.

O'Nolan worked as a civil servant, but he seems to have had considerable freedom to roam. The map of his daily route was well known. He might begin with an eye-opener at the Pearl before he moved over to the Scotch House by eleven or so each morning, later shifting to the bar at the Dolphin Hotel, where you could still get a good steak in wartime. He usually made a last stop at O'Rourke's in Blackrock where he lived, and often further delayed his return home with a game of cards and a bottle at a neighbor's house. (Though O'Nolan praised porter in "The Workmans Friend," he was devoted to his "ball o'malt.") Inasmuch as he greeted the day with a "curer" or three, it's astonishing he wrote anything at all, but the drink and the grind of the column ultimately dulled his talent and sapped his ambition. "A great future lay behind him," Hugh Kenner joked.

As O'Nolan's alcoholism progressed, so did his bedtime. Toward the end, his cronies carted him back to Blackrock and tucked him under the covers by the late afternoon. In spite of his notoriety as a columnist, he was afflicted with the familiar writerly complaint that his books had failed to generate the visibility and the money he craved and perhaps thought he deserved. ("I declare to God if I hear the word 'Joyce' again," he griped once, "I will surely froth at the gob!") Literary success on the grand scale did tap O'Nolan at last, partly through a postmodern affection for his quirky books, and partly because the creator of *Lost*, the hit television series, included a copy of *The Third Policeman* in a key scene. The novel soared onto Amazon's bestseller list, but the author was already in his grave, an irony he might have appreciated.

O'Nolan joined the gang at McDaids when it became a literary pub. The action focused on *The Bell*, a monthly journal with an office around the corner. Almost every afternoon, the contributors and the hangers-on showed up to shoot the bull, but no pub had enough room for so many sizable egos. Petty feuds of an irresolvable and sometimes unexplainable kind were bound to occur, such as the ongoing spat between O'Nolan and Kavanagh, who recognized each other's gifts and yet avoided any direct contact except to backbite. No doubt O'Nolan envied Kavanagh, who had a publisher in London and a reputation abroad, so he put down his rival as a country bumpkin, while Kavanagh sniffed at O'Nolan's inability to write a novel with the epic scope of *Moby-Dick*, a classic he admired.

In fact, Kavanagh was anything but a hick. Cronin cites him as McDaids' resident genius, possessed of a finely tuned sensibility that he kept hidden beneath a gruff exterior. Originally a farmer from County Monahan, he tried to support himself as a freelancer in Dublin while he wrote his poetry, and it sentenced him to a lifetime of poverty. His most memorable stint was as a cranky movie reviewer, who seldom sat through an entire film and expressed his dislike for Walt Disney. He survived instead on racetrack gambling, contributions from his brother Peter and a sympathetic clergyman, and loans from the Gnocchis, newsboys on Grafton Street. Kavanagh drank only stout initially, but he switched to whiskey as his frustrations mounted and his health declined, and it became his crutch, even his reason for being. The same was true of O'Nolan, who insisted that the choice lay between whiskey and boredom.

Kavanagh seemed never to tire of crossing swords with his adversary, but he often ran from the pub in disgust at the sight of Brendan Behan. He castigated Behan, some twenty years his junior, as a "phony and a blackguard," and he resented, as only a starving poet could, Behan's triumph as an international man of letters, honored for his plays and his memoirs and rich enough never to beg for another drink. On the other hand, Cronin found Behan wonderful company until he surrendered to the adulation, the liquor, and his private demons. Bisexual, with a taste for teenage boys and a long-suffering wife in the bargain, Behan bore all the hallmarks of a tortured soul, and he outdid the others in his undying affection for pubs.

Cronin tells of a Christmas Eve when he and Behan left McDaids and passed some carolers at Stephen's Green, who held up placards in support of a Christian charity. Behan despised the church and destroyed a placard in a fit of drunken pique, shouting, "Chairman Mao will soon put a stop to your fucking gallop, ye creepin' Jesus ye!" The carolers were too stunned to react, but four men from the crowd chased Behan, who scrambled over the the Green's spear-tipped iron fence to elude them. Only when the coast appeared to be clear did he emerge from the bushes, but his pursuers caught him and a brief scuffle ensued, after which Behan and Cronin bolted for the safety of the Russell Hotel's lobby. When the police arrived, Behan protested that he was the victim of some murderous country people, who might belong to a "rural-based organization with fascist tendencies."

Behan's brother Brian has recalled the time when Brendan rode a bus to Kilcoole to surprise J. P. Donleavy, the American-born author of *The Ginger Man* and another McDaids regular, with a visit. (There are four Ginger Man pubs in Texas and one in New York, each with the author's approval.) Nobody was at home, so Brendan climbed through a window and twiddled his thumbs until a desperate thirst overcame him. In a driving rain, he hiked to a pub about a mile away, but the hike left his shoes soaked, so he went back to Donleavy's to replace them. He found twenty-one pairs in a closet, stuffed them into a suitcase, and set off again, donning dry shoes as necessary and tossing the wet ones into a field.

"You'll have no bother finding them," he told his friend later. "Your first pair is just there over the fence and the rest of them every fifty yards or so up to the pub."

The Behan stories go on and on. When he was hungover, he blamed it on a bad pint—his twenty-seventh. Asked to reimburse a publican for a glass he broke, he balked at the ten-shilling price tag and cried, "Bless us and save us! Was it Waterford crystal?" No, the publican meant a *pane* of glass Behan had smashed during a brawl. Rather than buy a whole bottle of whiskey at closing time, afraid he'd forget where he'd stashed it the next morning, he once invested in a dozen expensive miniatures instead and planted two by the bed, two on a table, and so on. Behan often repeated an anecdote about an old man who drank two pints of poteen a day until he was sick, only to embark on the same routine as soon as he had recuperated. "When I've been off it for a fortnight," the old man explained, "I feel so good, I want to celebrate."

The anecdote could be applied to Behan himself. Predictably, his life ground to a crushing halt. The stories, once comic, turned tragic when he developed diabetes and failed in his many attempts to sober up. Racked with self-doubt, he became a cartoon character, red-faced and theatrically boisterous, yet he clung to his drinker's persona until the end, talking his books into a tape recorder rather than writing them. He died at forty-one— much earlier than O'Nolan (fifty-five) or Kavanagh (sixty-three), who lost a lung to cancer—but the public loved him despite his flaws, and he received the most fulsome Dublin funeral since the death of Michael Collins, the revolutionary and statesman. A statue at Mountjoy Prison, where his play *The Quare Fellow* is set, commemorates him, as does the Brendan Behan Pub in Jamaica Plain, Massachusetts, winner of the Guinness Perfect Pint Award in 1996.

McDaids isn't a literary pub anymore, but it looks much as it did during Behan's era. To reach the gents, you have to climb two perilous flights of stairs covered with a mottled blue carpet that might have been laid when the place opened in 1873. I pictured how animated it must have been with the *Bell* crowd around, but all I had for company was a trio of golfers from Atlanta, who'd just finished a round at the K Club in Kildere and were buying logo T-shirts before they returned to their rooms at the Westbury Hotel nearby. As enjoyable as McDaids can be, it's a tenderly curated museum piece now, not the hub of a distinct and vital community, and that's a fate it shares with so many of the trophy pubs in the city center, as I was beginning to understand.

The Traditional Music Archive on Merrion Square is just a short walk from McDaids. Here in Georgian splendor Yeats lived on the square for a time, as did Daniel O'Connell, the Liberator, who invested in his son's brewery in Cork and, as a Catholic, reaped the benefits of the backlash against Black Protestant Porter. At the archive, I hoped to gain an insight into what constituted real traditional music, so I turned to Ciaran Carson, the poet and musician, whose *Irish Traditional Music* is an indispensable guide. The book's appendix lists ten recommended CDs, and I found them all with the help of a librarian who also suggested a DVD compilation of old TV tapes before she installed me in front of a computer.

I watched the DVD first, glued to a performance by some men posing as "wrenboys." They were participating in an ancient ritual that still takes place in some towns on St. Stephen's Day, or December 26. They wore brightly colored costumes in orange, magenta, and puce, each apparently assembled from a rag bag, and their leader held a cage made of twigs atop which rested a wren, or a "wran" in Hiberno-English. Perhaps it had been hunted down for the ritual, but it looked stuffed to me, like a prop stored in a drawer from Christmas to Christmas. With a TV camera in tow, the boys marched into a house, where the leader launched an appeal for a donation:

The wran, the wran, the king of all birds
St. Stephen's Day was caught in the furze
Although he was little his family was great
So rise up, landlady, and give us a trate.
Up with the kettle and down with the pan
And give us a penny to bury the wran.

Next, a chubby wrenboy with a double chin stepped forward and squeezed the living daylights out of an accordion, stomping away until a subordinate jumped into the fray and added to the racket by banging on a bodhran.

The wrenboys were small beer, as it were, in contrast to some mummers from the Dublin suburb of Swords. The mummers wreak their merry havoc just after the holidays at the end of January, on St. Brigid's Eve, and they also dress in costume, although the fellows on my DVD hadn't gone to any great lengths to disguise themselves, merely sticking on fake beards, mustaches, and sideburns of the dime-store variety. They seemed determined to flaunt their reckless lack of ingenuity. They went from door to door, too, yelling "Mummers!" and putting on a disjointed playlet that again involved a plea for money. Each mummer represented a different character—the Prince, Buck Sweep, the Doctor, Devil a Doubt—and had a rhyme to speak and a specific role in the pageant. Some carried musical instruments, and they were noisier than the wrenboys.

After the mummers, I dived into the pile of CDs. Less than three bars into a Tommy Potts fiddle tune, I heard how moving, energetic, and energizing real traditional music can be. Potts, a

Dubliner, broke the rules and reinvented the fiddle, borrowing riffs from jazz and classical composers, and his peers admired him as an innovative virtuouso. Frankie Gavin, another wonderful fiddler who has jammed with Stéphane Grappelli, Earl Scruggs, and the Rolling Stones, once visited Potts, watched him play for a half hour, and never stopped crying. I listened to some tracks on Gavin's tribute album to Potts, then got lost in the sheer exuberance of a session recorded at the pub of Dan O'Connell (not the Liberator) in Knocknagree, County Cork, with Noel Hill on concertina and Tony McMahon on accordion. Set dancers had dished up a lively counterpoint by battering the timber floor with their shoes.

The melancholy ballads of Darach O'Cathain, a *sean-nos*, or "old style" performer in the a capella mode of Connemara, were very moving. He sang in Gaelic of love gone wrong, while Mary Ann Carolan had a clear, windswept voice that touched the heart, but it was Joe Cooley who packed the strongest emotional punch for me. Like McMahon, he played the accordion, much maligned in some quarters and ranked even lower than the suspect guitar. (An old joke goes: "How do you play the accordion?" Answer: "With a penknife.") Born in Peterswell, County Galway, Cooley hailed from a musical family—his parents both played the melodeon—and worked for a time as a builder, but he left for the U.S. in 1954 when he was about thirty and lived as a vagabond minstrel, supporting himself with gigs in New York, Boston, Chicago, and San Francisco, where the hippies revered him.

As Carson notes, Cooley employed the old-fashioned press-and-draw technique to dazzling effect, creating a unique sound that's been described as "lonesome." He was only recorded professionally once, at Lahiffe's Bar in his hometown just weeks before his death from cancer in 1973, and the photo on the CD shows a grinning, broad-chested youth with his head thrown back, as if to laugh in the face of every challenge, an attitude he kept until the end. "A lot of people around Ireland thought I was dead," he begins, and then pauses for effect before he adds, "a couple of times." Despite his illness, he rips through "The Blackthorn," a tune he learned from the Flanagan Brothers in the Catskills, with such skill, dexterity, speed, and fire that I almost disturbed the archive's equilibrium with some whoops and yelps of appreciation.

Even at a distance, you could sense the music binding everyone together at Lahiffe's in a form of *duende*, that power Lorca defined as springing out of energetic instinct. "Whatever has black sounds has *duende*," he quoted Manuel Torres, the great Andalusian singer. I kept those words in mind when I left for the Brazen Head on a beautiful evening in early August, marred ever so slightly by a chilly foretaste of autumn. The weather can affect a pub's handle, as Kevin Hynes once told me. Before the grim, unrelenting rain of June and July, Ireland had logged an unseasonably dry and mild April, and business at McSorley's had dropped off, but the wet months had driven people back indoors and rewarded Kevin with some bumper profits.

From Ranelagh I rode the LUAS tram, inevitably known as the Daniel Day, to Stephen's Green and strolled down Grafton Street through the last shoppers hunting for bargains until I reached the Liffey, where a lovely wash of twilight fell on the water. Closer to the pub, I caught the scent of roasted barley drifting over from the Guinness brewery at St. James's Gate. Two Japanese youths stood on a bench outside the Brazen Head and took photos of the stone walls and battlements with their cell phones, and probably beamed the images to their friends at the Irish Pub Company's branch in Tokyo or Kyoto. That scenario, once the material of science fiction, didn't seem so far-fetched anymore.

Two of the pub's three rooms are used for music, and the smaller one was thick with tourists—Italian, French, Swedish, and others—camped out around a little stage, although I saw no cops or firemen, at least in uniform. As for frat boys, I met two from Colorado, beefy guys with the look of second-string football players, who had already signed a dollar bill and handed it over to be tacked up. They were thrilled to be in Ireland and swore they'd drink as much beer as they could possibly hold, and I was reminded, in a sentimental way, of my former self, the romantic naïf from California.

The music started at nine thirty on the dot. That was so contrary to the disregard of the Irish for punctuality, their refusal to accept the concept of time as anything other than arbitrary, it raised a red flag. A quartet of musicians, very groomed compared to the frazzled, apocalyptic look of the Dubliners, stepped onto the stage and tuned up—*two* guitars, a banjo, and a bodhran player who doubled on the bones, once made from animal ribs but generally wooden now. There was a hush in the room, a muted air of anticipation such as you register in church before the start of a sermon. When the quartet struck its first chord, some members of the audience, unable to contain themselves, clapped along as if by rote, well before the music had a chance to rouse their passions, perhaps as suggested by a guidebook.

The group on stage was even less traditional than the one at the Oliver St. John Gogarty. Without a doubt, they lacked Joe

Cooley's fire, and the black sounds were missing from their repertoire. They were competent and possessed a folksy authority, but I felt no emotional connection. They resembled a tepid version of the Irish musicians from my college days—the Clancy Brothers, say, who were on the jukebox in every New York pub in the 1960s and struck the spark for many a party. Cooley's internal focus, the way he appeared to be isolated in his own world, oblivious of the crowd and attentive only to the dictated notes as they pulsed through him—that was missing. Cooley was an artist while these musicians appeared to be professional entertainers, and though they failed to meet my newly evolved standard of authenticity, they satisfied the expectations of the crowd.

In the end, I wrote off the Brazen Head as another museum piece, and wondered if a night at the Brazen Head in Brooklyn—or San Francisco, Omaha, or Mingo, West Virginia—would have been very different. Had Ireland already been packaged so completely that it could never be unwrapped? The thought was so unsettling I stopped for a whiskey at Davy Byrnes, another trophy and also Joyce's "moral pub," where the eponymous owner frowned on gambling. You won't find anyone scrounging for tips now, though, nor would Joyce recognize the place, lavishly refurbished as an Art Deco jewel the year after he left Dublin for good. The pub is very smart and popular with foreigners, who can order Leopold Bloom's lunch—a gorgonzola sandwich and a glass of burgundy—for about fifteen dollars during the summer high season.

Chapter 6

THE GRAVEDIGGERS

M Y NIGHT ON the town, though not without its aspects of fun, taught me I couldn't count on the trophy pubs of the city center for a taste of unspoiled tradition. As usual, the easy solution I'd hoped for—the Brazen Head as a Platonic ideal, that is—had evaporated and left me with the not-so-easy job of extending the search to areas of Dublin where the tourists seldom go. In essence, the trophies could be divided into two camps: those like Gogarty's that deliver a packaged, formulaic Irish experience, and others such as McDaids and Davy Byrnes that don't actively court visitors from abroad and yet are inundated, anyway, for literary, historical, or sentimental reasons. The high-profile pubs are just too adulterated by folks like me to qualify, plus they represent a costly investment that doesn't leave much room for ragged edges.

The Brazen Head belongs to John Hoyne and Tom Maguire, I learned from the *Sunday Business Post*, who bought it for about $8 million in 2004. Maguire has been in the game for twenty-two years and had sold about five pubs in the previous three, leapfrogging in the manner of Dessie Hynes, perhaps to fund the purchase of a trophy without borrowing heavily. The tactic is more common than ever now, and it's carried out on a grander scale. While individuals or small partnerships still run most pubs, they often have a finger in many different pies. Maguire has an interest in two other pubs, for example, so his attention is necessarily divided in the way of Frank Smyth, but he's not spread as thinly as the high roller publican Charlie Chawke, whose interests also include property development and a piece of the Sunderland UK football team.

Chawke owns the Goat in Goatstown, County Dublin, where Gertie, a real goat later released into the mountains, once acted as a mascot. (Gertie's kids were Dinny, Miley, and Biddy, and a statue of her stands at the pub, in Gogarty-esque splendor.) Chawke has the Dropping Well on the Dodder River, too, used as a hospital during the famine, and he paid about $29 million in 2005 for the Old Orchard in a suburb that's being redeveloped. "It's basically being seen as a building site," he has said, and he's turned down several substantial offers from developers. The planning board rejected his own scheme to construct 114 apartments, shops, office and light industrial units, and a medical center on the land. As part of a broad investment portfolio, such pubs are under pressure to produce.

Louis Fitzgerald is an even heavier hitter. He has about twenty-four pubs across Dublin, Kildare, and Galway and an estimated worth of $170 million, all cultivated from the single acorn of a rundown joint on Townsend Street that he picked up for a song in 1970, financing the deal with a bank loan. When he acquired the Stag's Head recently, a city center trophy that dates from 1760 and sports an antlered buck on a wall of the listed building it occupies, he dropped about $8.5 million at auction, although he'd just seen the pub for the first time. The Stag's Head had a "no TV except for special events" policy, but it's not rigidly enforced anymore, and Fitzgerald has opened a cellar bar for music on the weekends. The purchase was no apparent strain on his finances, because he shelled out about $54 million for the Arlington Hotel by O'Connell Bridge on the Liffey that same year. The Arlington's bars and nightclub are catnip to believers in Fairytale Ireland, with their "hooleys," or boozy parties, and a Riverdance-style floorshow.

The Thomas Read Group comes at the business from a different, trendier angle, and has the young, the hip, and the fair as its target. Its gem is the elegant Bailey across from Davy Byrnes, the site of many famous quarrels and disastrous affairs, and the group also owns Ron Blacks (champagne bar, live jazz); Searsons on Upper Baggot Street, a magnet for yuppies; and the lushly renovated Lincolns Inn near the National Gallery. Bars based on a foreign theme also figure in the group's holdings—Bodega with a Spanish twist, Pravda with a Russian one, and the glitzy Floridita, where you can savor a "modern cocktail" on the patio and smoke an "exclusive" Habanero cigar. Floridita makes the idea of a quiet pint sound positively quaint.

Some Dubliners greet such cosmopolitan sophistication eagerly, and while there's no denying that good craic can be had at the pubs of Chawke, Fitzgerald, and the Read Group, the owners can't possibly exercise a Birchall-like quality control over them all. The personal touch may go begging. Each pub is especially vulnerable to the bottom line, too, and if one fails to perform, it could be divested in the way of Ranelagh's Four Provinces or Quinlans in suburban Terenure, sold for $12.5 million to provide the ground for thirty-seven apartments and a parking lot. "There are publicans and there are businessmen," Graham Canning of the Kestrel in Walkinstown once told the *Post*. "Publicans are not going to succeed." The pub trade isn't about drink and talk anymore, Canning felt. Instead you sell product, service, atmosphere, and entertainment at the right price—just as the IPC does.

That amounts to a drastic change in attitude, because most pubs in Ireland have always been family-owned and operated. A decade ago, nine out of ten met this criterion, but it's no longer the case in the city. Still, there are over ninety pubs in the Republic that have been in the same family for at least a hundred years, although only two or three are in County Dublin, among them John Kavanagh. It's located next to a gate of Glasnevin Cemetery, wittily referred to as the city's "dead center" and "Croak Park" after the GAA stadium nearby. Daniel O'Connell and his followers established Glasnevin as a burial ground for Catholics, but it accepts the deceased of any faith now and honors O'Connell with a 165-foot-high round tower by his tomb. For company, he has such luminaries as Michael Collins, Brendan Behan, Éamon de Valera, and Gerard Manley Hopkins, lonely and secluded in Ireland, who is interred in a plot reserved for Jesuits.

I got wind of John Kavanagh by chance when I ducked into the Barge, a pub on the Grand Canal, to avoid being drenched in a sudden late-summer downpour. Swans glide by the Barge on occasion, but there's no other aspect of romance. It's a generic place without any maritime flavor, and its two TVs were blabbing the news to a bored bunch of patrons, one of whom might well have been a truly heroic pintman. He looked the part, at any rate, with rubicund cheeks, pouchy eyes, a potbelly, and a bemused expression that long hours on a barstool seem to produce. If a bomb had exploded inside the Barge, I doubt that he would have shifted a haunch. He was in a talkative mood, too, although not in a bellicose or intrusive way. Instead he acted light-hearted and guileless, as if by emptying out the contents of his brain he'd be doing everybody in the vicinity a world of good.

When he heard my accent, he jumped on it and asked where in America I was from, secretly hoping, I soon realized, I'd say New York, Boston, or Philadelphia, the three cities he'd visited himself, so that the anecdotes he proceeded to tell anyway would have a superior degree of relevance. It's a point of pride with the Irish to have been to the U.S., and they're adept at separating their admiration for our culture from their revulsion over our foreign policy. The first anecdote concerned a cheesesteak sandwich and doesn't bear repeating, but the second was better. He'd attended a Mets game with a cousin from Queens, paid an extortionate price for a beer, and caught a foul ball with his bare hands.

"Mike Piazza," he gloated.

"Amazing." How else to respond?

He kept the ball on a bookshelf at home, he confided. His cousin, not Piazza, had autographed it. He liked Ashtons pub in Clonskeagh down the road, he added, and he'd be heading for it right now if he didn't have such a gorgeous pint before him. He spoke of it very lovingly, as though the pint had landed there by accident, a gift from the gods, and then wondered if the Barge was my local. I took this as an accusation, denied it vehemently, and outlined the nature of my quest, even alluding to *The Quiet Man* and Pat Cohan's, and when I was done, he slapped the bar for emphasis and cried, "The Gravediggers!" the nickname for John Kavanagh. It was on the north side of the Liffey, he went on, and far from the tourist trail. The Kavanaghs, who were purists, hadn't altered or remodeled it in over a century.

I chose to check on the information, of course, unwilling to trust the word of a pintman who'd been drinking at the Barge, maybe for weeks, and saw that he hadn't exaggerated. According to *The Story of the Irish Pub*, John Kavanagh occupies the former residence of John O'Neill, a hotelier, who began to serve alcohol in 1833, the year after Glasnevin's inception, and earned a tidy bundle on grief-stricken mourners. When his daughter Suzanne married John Kavanagh two years later, O'Neill gave him the pub, and the couple begat twenty-five children, as the Bible has it, and launched a dynasty, including three sons who fought for the Union Army during the Civil War and were all commended for bravery at the Battle of Gettysburg. Eugene Kavanagh, the current publican, represented the sixth generation in charge.

I set off for Kavanagh's on a fine September afternoon, as Kerry prepared to tackle Cork in the GAA All-Ireland Final, or championship match, before a crowd of some eighty-two thousand at Croke Park. (Gaelic football combines elements of both soccer and rugby, and it's as fast-paced as hurling, the oldest Irish game that's played with a stick and a ball and dates back to 1272.) As a typical southsider, I was guilty of being provincial and only crossed the Liffey to see a movie on O'Connell Street or a play at the Abbey Theatre, so I looked forward to exploring the area. The north side is often described as "working class," but that has always sounded inaccurate to me and even insulting. There are more apartment blocks, to be sure, and more enclaves of recent immigrants, but you could as easily speak of the grand houses on Griffith Avenue and the North Circular Road, or the choice sea-side districts of Clontarf and Howth.

The area reminded me of London's Islington, also a northern borough, where I'd lived for a time. Islington's population is a wild blend of races, colors, and creeds, left-leaning, progressive, and more vital because of it. The wealthy south side of Dublin can be staid and even stuffy, rather full of itself, so it lacks the vi-brant polyglot street life of the north side—of Moore Street, say, where the Irish equivalent of Cockney vendors hawk their bar-gain fruit and vegetables from carts. The butchers still sell cheap cuts of meat, too, the kidney and tongue, oxtail and liver that are scarce in Ranelagh, and they're ringed by Russian, Polish, and African groceries, and also by noodle shops that herald an upstart Chinatown.

Everywhere I looked people were on the move. The sidewalks in front of all the pubs were already awash with football jerseys, the green-and-gold of Kerry and the red of Cork. On Gardiner Street, I skirted the fringe of Monto, the old brothel district, where the madams operated freely until 1925. The authorities were so le-nient that they earned a citation for their tolerance in the Britan-nica of 1903. "Dublin furnishes an exception to the usual practice in the United Kingdom in that the city police permit 'open houses' that carried on more publicly than even in the south of Europe or Algeria," the entry read, scarcely a feather in the cap of local government. About sixteen hundred prostitutes worked in Monto at its peak between 1860 and 1900, sometimes sold into what amounted to slavery by their hungry parents.

The most humanely treated women were confined to "flash houses" for wealthy swells, who paid a fee to be admitted and had to pass muster with the bouncers, or "fancy men," hired to keep out the undesirables. Flash houses could be graciously furnished, often with a piano in the parlor and the madam's name inscribed on a fanlight above the hall door as an advertisement. Such madams bragged that their girls were disease-free, and they posted medical certificates to that effect—supplied by their doctor clients—over the beds. For the small tradesmen and the office drones, there was a second tier of brothels, clean and functional but not so well appointed, where women who'd become pregnant and fallen from grace at flash houses were sometimes employed. The kips were the lowest tier of all, situated in grungy tenements and staffed with streetwalkers past their prime, who were condemned to service filthy, clap-ridden soldiers and sailors.

There were pubs, of course, such as Joe O'Reilly, Paddy Clare, and Jack Maher, where the women sat outside in warm weather to show off their wares. Becky Cooper, who ran a kip house, drank at the Leinster Arms across from it until she was barred, an insult she did not take lightly, protesting instead by breaking the pub's windows with her shoes. In spite of her outbursts, Becky was always well dressed, wore long hair down to her shoulders, and had a reputation for being kind-hearted compared to May Oblong, as hard as coal, who'd slash you up with a bacon knife if you gave her any reason. May forced her girls to stand in the freezing rain to flirt and tease, and issued beatings to those who disobeyed her orders, covering them with bruises and giving them black eyes. Far more respected was Annie Mack, who entertained the Prince of Wales, later King Edward VII. Shy of publicity, he slipped into her brothel through secret tunnels beneath Montgomery Street.

In Monto, James Joyce soaked up the material for what became the "Nighttown" chapter of *Ulysses*, and was such a regular visitor that his pal Gogarty chided him about it in a limerick.

> There is a young fellow named Joyce,
> Who possesses a sweet tenor voice.
> He goes down to the kips
> With a psalm on his lips,
> And biddeth the harlots rejoice.

I arrived at my destination too early for a pint, so I strolled through Glasnevin Cemetery instead and found it very amiable for such a thought-provoking spot, handsomely landscaped with mature trees, even some California redwoods, and paths that wind through the necropolis and attract elderly cyclists perhaps shopping for a plot. Along the outer walls, there were some bleak guard towers that once kenneled a pack of vicious Cuban bloodhounds, who were let loose at night to scare off "resurrectionists," or graverobbers. The robbers earned a pretty penny selling corpses to medical students and schools in the nineteenth century, often unearthing one by tying a rope around its neck and giving it a hard yank. The relatives of the departed, understandably upset, stood watch over a grave or resorted to a tamper-proof iron coffin.

Considering John Kavanagh's location, a few corpses must have landed on its doorstep over the years. Under the Coroners Act of 1846, any coroner had the right to dispatch a dead body to the closest pub, and the proprietor was obliged to store it, usually in a cool cellar with the kegs of beer, until an inquest could be held. The law stayed on the books until 1962 and encouraged some publicans to wear a second hat as undertakers. There are still pubs that advertise the service, such as Doyles in Urlingford, County Kilkenny, where I once eased a parched throat on a long trip to West Cork. The word "undertaker" was appended to a sign out front, but no cadavers were stored below, a blonde barmaid assured me, because the mortuary magic was performed in a parlor down the block.

From Glasnevin I walked to sleepy Prospect Square, where John Kavanagh is the only business. The storefront, a deep shade of red, contrasts with the cold gray cement of O'Neill's old house. The pub has two doors, and the first led me into a lounge bar so ordinary I could have been in Detroit, Atlanta, or pretty much anywhere else. I cursed the pintman at the Barge, who was obviously in cahoots with the author of *The Story of the Irish Pub* and had sent me on a wild-goose chase. The room's only hint of tradition resided in its only customer, an antiquated fellow— probably a cemetery cyclist—who wore a suit, a tie, and a tweed cap. Irish gents of a certain age dress like that every day, as if their failure to do so would cause a sharp rupture in the fabric of civilization.

A noise distracted me. It came from the other side of the wall, so I stepped out and went through the second door, where a parallel universe awaited me. Here, in fact, was the fabled Gravediggers, with its original bar still intact, untouched since the 1830s and crammed with animated drinkers, both men and women, who were divided into small knots by some panels that once had sectioned off a grocery counter. (The lounge was added in 1980, and it's used mostly as a dining room.) Miracle of miracles, there was no TV and nobody complaining about its absence despite the All-Ireland Final, nor did I hear any recorded music, just the low babble of voices in discourse, as comforting as the Tolka River rippling through Glasnevin on its way to the Botanic Gardens.

The single room was compact and convivial, its floor almost black with age. Dimly lit, it felt conspiratorial, although not in an oppressive sense. The Gravediggers isn't exclusive. If a stranger hunts it down, he or she joins the conspiracy, too, and relishes the sweet satisfaction of discovering a semi-secret hide-away. I could imagine myself bragging about it, lording it over my friends. "Never been to the Gravediggers?" I'd ask. "What a pity!" Hard benches provide the seating, and the pints are much cheaper than in Ranelagh. For heat, the pub has a cast-iron fireplace, and for amusement an antique ring-toss game, but talk was clearly the drawing card. There was no bric-a-brac anywhere, either, phony or otherwise, only wood and more wood burnished and abraded over time. If you introduced a scrap of plastic, it might burst into flame.

Eugene Kavanagh, the licensee since 1973, lives above the pub with his wife, Kathleen, and his son Niall, the last of his six children, a barman informed me. I was more curious than ever about Kavanagh and why he was so resistant to change, valuing tradition over modern cocktails and exclusive cigars. Did he fear that he'd lose some quality integral to Ireland's identity, that ineffable something I'd first experienced at Birchall's? I wanted to ask him, but he wasn't around, and the barman was too frantic to field any more questions. The GAA match had just ended with Kerry on top, and a band of excited jersey-clad fans were streaming into the Gravediggers, so I sat on a hard bench and drank my pint, vowing to catch up with Kavanagh next Saturday.

Not long after my trip to the north side, I came across an odd news item about the Quiet Man Movie Club, based in Cork. Its members are guardians of the true flame, determined to build a Quiet Man pub in Cong, the film's location. John Ford would have preferred to shoot it in Spiddal, County Galway, his father's birthplace—both his parents were native speakers of Gaelic, who had emigrated to the U.S.—but he failed to get his way. He fared better with the film's budget, though. Herbert Yates, the head of Republic Pictures, kept a tight hold on the pursestrings until Ford dragged him to a wild and scenic stretch of Connemara and pointed out a cottage—whitewashed, naturally, with shutters and a thatched roof.

"There it is, the house where I was born," he said, as the tears rolled down his cheeks. Yates began to cry, too, and replied, "Okay, you can have the $1.5 million for your picture."

Ford loved to tell the story, since in reality he'd been born John Martin Feeney in Cape Elizabeth, Maine. Still, he treasured his Irish roots, and his "beautiful travelogue" has had a more profound, widespread, and lasting impact of the public's vision of Ireland than I'd orginally thought. When the movie was released on video in 1985, for example, it sold about a quarter of a million copies in the UK alone in the first five years, despite the fact that it played frequently on television. Its influence on the Irish Tourist Board, founded in 1952, the same year as *The Quiet Man*'s theatrical release, was monumental. The board adopted Ford's bucolic imagery for its ads, and the look of the film became the look of the Emerald Isle.

The vision of the country as a pastoral refuge is still so prevalent that such keen-eyed observers as Thomas Friedman of the *New York Times* have remarked on it. "People all over the world are looking to Ireland for its reservoir of sprituality," Friedman once wrote, "hoping to siphon off what they can to save their souls." Critics harp on about the soul of U2, and the soulful performances of Van Morrison. (Even Angel of *Buffy* fame, born in Ireland in 1727, has a soul, but it's a hindrance to him because he's a vampire.) *The Quiet Man* may contribute to the success of such companies as Creative Irish Gifts, whose mail order catalog of 2002—Guinness T-shirts, claddagh rings, flashing shamrock pins—generated $13 million on the merchandise, some of it manufactured in China.

For the Quiet Man Movie Club, the pub project in Cong sounded like a mission. (You can already wet your whistle at Quiet Man pubs in Melbourne, Paris, Boston, and Dover, New Jersey.) Pat Cohan's still stands in the village, but it's not identical to the pub in the film. Ford liked the storefront of Johnny Murphy's grocery better, so he transferred Cohan's sign to it. As for the pub interiors, they were shot on a Hollywood sound stage, and the props and fittings had been stored in an L.A. warehouse for more than fifty years. The club was rumored to have purchased the lot, and intended to ship it across the Atlantic and reassemble it as a tourist attraction—the authenticity of replication taken to the max.

In the old days, before JVC excavators made the gravediggers at Glasnevin obsolete, they'd knock on an outside wall of John

Kavanagh when they wanted a pint, and a small boy carried out the beer and collected their money if they had any, or marked it down to credit on his pad. That was Eugene Kavanagh. Because the pub is so ancient, I pictured Eugene as a relatively decrepit sort, pale and short of breath from his long career in the haze and fumes, but he bounded down the stairs to meet me when I stopped by on Saturday, as fit as a man can be at sixty-eight. He's short, stocky, and pugnacious, an obsessive runner who has competed in 169 marathons—Beijing, Paris, Boston, he's circled the globe—along with more strenuous events such as a hundred-mile race across the Sierra Nevada at the height of summer and a Belfast-to-Dublin jaunt.

Kavanagh's face looked familiar, and I realized I might have seen it before on an officer of the law, friendly but a trifle wary, quick to size someone up, and hinting that serious trouble lay ahead if you crossed him. He wouldn't be the type to suffer fools gladly. He wasn't eager to talk at first, either. He might bar television from the pub, but he has one in his quarters and devotes his Saturday afternoons to horseracing and other sports. I offered to call later in the week and arrange a more convenient time, but that wouldn't do. His phone is unlisted, and he never gives out the number of his cell. Even the Gravediggers doesn't have a listed phone.

"I'm eccentric," Eugene said, with a tight grin, and set about proving it. Instead of going back upstairs, he stood at the bar and talked with me for three straight hours.

He was proud of the Gravediggers, having rescued it from the brink of disaster after he bought it from John M. Kavanagh, his stepfather and a man he revered, who'd grown old and tired and only opened in the evenings because of a depressed economy. His own father, Michael, a carpenter and John M.'s brother, had died when Eugene was just eight and left the family so destitute that Eugene spent two-and-a-half years in an orphanage before his mother married again—to John M. this time, making him both a nephew and a stepson. He was put right to work at the pub, but he didn't mind. The Christian Brothers had taught him discipline, along with manners and respect. They were tough but fair, he said, and he'd never been abused, even though he was a "little blondie fella" and a favorite "on the bell," charged with answering the door and calling a brother to the phone.

He had to cut back on his pub chores, though, when he accepted a job with Guinness as a boy laborer at fifteen. You had to sit for a special exam to be hired, and he was fortunate to pass it, since all he did at home was eat, sleep, and play football. "It must have been my mother's prayers that did the trick," he ventured, although she relied on other forms of motivation, too, and gave him the odd larruping to cure him of his bad temper and his pig-headedness. He stayed with Guinness for nineteen years, eventually moving into the adult work force, and loved it. "I'd have died for that company," he swore, but that was before Diageo had taken over.

Diageo was a sore point with Eugene, and its mere mention set him off. He sold more stout per square foot than any bar in Dublin, he claimed, and yet he felt shabbily treated. The accountants and merchandisers were in control now, and they knew nothing about the pub business, he said, and seemed to have no interest in learning. The company's attitude toward service was indifferent, he thought, and it reflected a similar indifference among publicans, especially the absentee owners. Rather than paying attention to the basics, the pubs aligned with the leisure industry and cooked up gimmicks to survive—quiz nights with cash prices, Texas Hold 'Em tournaments, bingo, karaoke, I'd seen them all myself—and if they kept it up, they'd drift even farther from their traditional function as a space apart for socializing, where casual friendships and a democratic spirit prevail.

Greed had the Irish in its grip, Eugene believed, despite their high level of intelligence. He wasn't entirely sympathetic to the new Ireland, nor was he shy about making it known. Snobbery and pettiness were afoot, he asserted, with people trying to outdo the neighbors and envying someone else's material success. They wanted everything handed to them on a silver platter, as well. Nobody expected their children to be plumbers, carpenters, or plasterers anymore, even though those trades paid good wages. Instead, the kids had to be professionals—doctors, lawyers, brokers—and drive a flashy car and buy a pricey house in the suburbs. He spoke in a measured tone without any rancor, giving voice to an opinion only beginning to be heard above a whisper—that Ireland's sudden prosperity might have a downside.

Kavanagh also had strong opinions about being a publican. "It helps if it's bred into you. It's not my job," he insisted, seconding Dessie Hynes. "It's my life." To do it right, you need a small, manageable unit, where the owner is around all the time and accepts full responsibility for every aspect of the trade, from training the staff to schmoozing with the regulars. "If you're willing to do that," he told me, "you can earn a very good living." He'd been able to buy up an entire block of Prospect Square himself, currently worth a small fortune, but he felt sheepish just saying that. He didn't have a clue what to do with so much money—security had always been his goal. The pub was also worth a bundle, but he wouldn't have sold it even if his kids had begged off—and luckily they hadn't. Instead, he'd have put it in a trust.

"I'm a preservationist," Eugene said, and a part of what he pre- serves are his memories. There was his grandmother Josie, for in- stance, a strong woman who frightened the bejesus out of him in her black widow's weeds, worn long after her husband John H. Kavanagh had died. Her nose was a hooked beak, and she leaned on a cane on account of her varicose veins. "I thought she was a witch," Eugene laughed, "but I was only four." John H. had suf- fered from "the nerves," calmed them with liquor, and hastened his early demise, and that was one reason, along with an addictive personality, that Eugene himself has never drunk any alcohol. I must have looked at him strangely, because he corrected himself. "No, no, twice I took a drink for medicinal purposes, some hot whiskey when I was sick in bed with the flu. I hated it, but I felt fine by the morning. I've only missed two half-days of work at the pub in my life."

A fellow at the bar cleared his throat and interrupted us. He hadn't visited Kavanagh's for a while and shared a memory of his own, although he didn't have complete faith in it. He nodded toward a dark corner and asked if a coffin hadn't rested there in the past. "No, but you might have seen that in a fil-um," Eugene informed him, since the pub had once been used as a movie set. The man seemed disappointed, so Eugene cheered him up with a spot of trivia and explained that the term "jar," meaning a pint, had been coined at the Gravediggers during World War I, when a shortage of pint glasses forced the barmen to rely on jam jars as substitutes.

By virtue of living over the pub, Eugene was at the mercy of his customers, but he swears it isn't a hardship. When he's relaxing upstairs, he's perfectly at ease unless he senses a weird vibration down below, like a dip in the barometric pressure, and that's the signal for him to show his face. If there's an argument or a dust-up, he prefers to resolve it himself instead of calling the police. He was a boxer in his youth and never lost a match, except once when he gulped down ten pints of water to gain some pounds and go up a weight class, and he played indoor soccer until he was fifty-nine. If you took into account the marathons, too, and that penetrating gaze, you'd think twice before you violated the barroom etiquette at the Gravediggers.

His oldest son, Anthony, a banker, would most likely become the publican when Eugene threw in the towel. Ciaran, another son, who'd been a chef in Italy for eight years, had taken over and improved the pub's cuisine, and served both lunch and dinner in the lounge with the help of his sister Anne. (Though opinionated, Eugene's no Luddite who's against progress.) Niall, at twenty-five, is the apple of his father's eye, a smiling, good-natured young man with Down syndrome, who still pulls pints and has been a champion swimmer, specializing in the butterfly. "He brought unity and happiness to this house," Eugene said, as Niall passed by and paused to greet the regulars.

He remembered when Niall was born, and how he had dropped Kathleen at the hospital around midnight, chose not to stay, and returned to Prospect Square. He received a call early the next morning to report that both the mother and child were doing fine, but he got a second call later from a doctor, who urged him to come in right away. He knew something must be wrong, and when he saw the baby he knew what it was, yet he and Kathleen, who believe in the hereafter, decided Niall must have been sent to them for a reason. Only once did Eugene crack, a month after the birth. He drove to Portmarnock by the sea and cried and cried, but he came to an acceptance of the facts and never looked back.

For Niall's sixteenth birthday, he gave the boy a racehorse—a six-week-old foal that only cost him three grand. Eugene owns some horses himself, all jumpers bred for the National Hunt, but he doesn't bet on them because gambling, like drink, can be addictive. Though Niall can't really read and has a limited vocabulary, Eugene invited him to name the foal. "Rory," Niall suggested, but that was the name of a dog they once had and not inventive enough. A few days later, Niall called his father outside and pointed toward the sky at twilight and shouted, "Sunset!" so they agreed on Rory's Sunset. The expectations were low for such a cheap purchase, but Rory's Sunset won a maiden hurdle and next a handicap hurdle for a bigger purse, after which someone offered $125,000 for the horse, but Niall turned it down.

The afternoon had slipped by, and we were finally talked out. I watched a last ray of sunshine explode through the pub's front windows and ignite the rich gold color of the ceiling. There were about twenty people at the bar, and they each had three personalities, Eugene joked—sober, half-sober, and pissed. Kathleen came down to let him know his dinner was ready, and he puffed up in her presence. "She paints, she teaches, she writes poetry," he whispered, afraid that he'd embarrass her by going on. He advised me to look at a painting of hers in the lounge before I left. For the first time, he sounded a bit unconfident, even slightly apologetic. "I'm totally different to the norm," he said, almost with a sigh, as if to sum up our conversation. "I can't help it. It's just me."

At Birchall's, where I stopped on my way home, the renovation had begun, but the pub remained open in spite of it, with building materials scattered here and there. The old slate floor was gone, and so were the carpets. The clutter had disappeared, creating more space and visibility. The dodgy rear entrance had been fixed—a boon to those who liked to slip out via a side street rather than into the bright lights of Ranelagh Road. Half the banquettes were stripped of their upholstery and covered in slick, mocha-colored leather, with little stools, still perfect for milkmaids, to match. A mild chemical odor, that mix of paint and sealants and flooring compound, wafted over everything. Newness was the smell of Birchall's now, and maybe of Ireland.

Eugene Kavanagh's comments about Diageo had the ring of prophecy when I read the *Irish Independent* at the bar. A lead story in the business section addressed the firm's problems with its Guinness brand at home. In 2001, the Irish consumed 70 percent of their alcohol in pubs, but the figure had dropped to 47 percent, and the cheap lagers at off-licenses—so cheap some publicans were buying from supermarkets at a better price than their wholesalers offered—and the growing popularity of wine did not bode well for stout. Reportedly, Diageo intended to sell its landmark complex at St. James's Gate and move to an industrial park in the suburbs—a wise financial decision, perhaps, but one that would cost Dublin a precious piece of its history. It would be a different city without that scent of roasted barley along the Liffey.

As the pace of change in Ireland quickened, Kavanagh's decision to preserve his family pub and its memories acquired a sort of nobility. He wasn't so much stuck in the past as choosing to occupy a middle ground between his heritage and the future, refusing to swap the traditional values he believed in for a passel of unknowns. In the headlong rush toward material gain that had captivated so many of the Irish, the middle ground had largely been passed over and ignored. Even Ireland's ancient treasures, such as the Hill of Tara in County Meath, where the legendary high kings once ruled, had lost its sacred glow in the current climate.

Tara is the dwelling place of the ancient pagan gods, and an entrance to the mythical otherworld. With its megalithic tomb, its barrows and fortifications, and the standing stone called Lia Fail, or Stone of Destiny, said to roar at the touch of Tara's rightful king, it's the equal of Delphi or Stonehenge, yet the government planned to build a highway near it that might intrude upon an archaeological site of immense value. The plan had provoked an outcry, not only in Ireland but around the world, over the desecration of such a vital site, and it had prompted Seamus Heaney to accuse the Celtic Tiger of smashing the strings of the Irish harp with its tail. Tara represents "an ideal of the spirit," Heaney said, and its savage destruction "is a signal that the priorities on these islands have changed."

Chapter 7

THE HALCYON DAYS
OF MANHOOD

BEFORE I MOVED to Ranelagh, while in my brief court-
ing phase, I rented a short-term furnished apartment in
wealthy Ballsbridge, although my place belonged to the lower
depths of the housing market. The real estate agent described it
as "twee," and its three petite rooms, adorned with knick-knacks
and needlepoint samplers, needed only a Thomas Kinkade print
to be terminally cute. (*Emerald Isle Cottage* is included in
Kinkade's vast gallery of prints. "To me, Ireland means tradition
and stability," he says on his Web site, suggesting he hasn't visited
the real Emerald Isle for a while.) To escape from the heart-
shaped throw pillows and the ceramic angels on a shelf, each with
its hands clasped in prayer, I walked almost daily along the Dodder River, still a lively urban trout stream, past the rugby stadium
on Landsdowne Road and then Shelbourne Park, where the
greyhounds run, to Ringsend on the river's bank.

After my trip to John Kavanagh and the north side, I retraced
the familiar route, convinced now that I was more likely to find
traditional pubs in those neighborhoods where pistachio oil hadn't

yet arrived. Ringsend qualifies handsomely in that respect. It has no "destination" restaurants, only a small café, a chip shop, and Good View Chinese, a takeaway place. There are no video stores, either, and no supermarkets, just one master butcher and a mom-and-pop grocery with giant turnips and huge bundles of kale out front in season. The presence of Paddy Power and Ladbrokes, two bookie joints filled with ardent punters, was another encouraging sign, and so, too, was Cecil's Barbershop, a trig red and white building where senior citizens availed themselves of budget haircuts three days a week.

Here was the home territory of the notoriously thirsty dockers, and though the new high-rise apartments and office blocks have altered the face of the quays on the Liffey, Ringsend retains a trace of the seaman's salty swagger. The village grew up around St. Patrick's Roman Catholic Church, where two streets converge to form a hub. The city center may be only a mile away, but Ringsend feels enclosed, apart, an entity onto itself. It has no shortage of pubs. Clustered on one street are the Raytown Bar, Hobblers End, and the Oarsman, while on the other the Yacht and Sally's Return stand almost side by side, their windows bedecked with model ships and ropes hitched into the panoply of knots featured in sailor's manuals.

Indeed, Ringsend had served as Dublin's port in the early 1700s, when packet boats from England tied up offshore. Passengers boarded a smaller craft to reach the city, or used a Ringsend Car, horse-drawn and able to negotiate the Dodder's mudflats at low tide, although the journey was scarcely salutary. "It is one of the most horrible stinks of filth I ever beheld," wrote a reluctant visitor. "Every house swarmed with ragged, squalid tenancy, and dung and garbage lay in heaps." Crime was rampant, especially around villainous Beggars Bush, a hill overlooking Dublin Bay, where thieves and other scoundrels watched and waited for travelers. With five main roads to pillage, the highwaymen pursued their quarry so skillfully that the locals carried arms at night. The Brennans, a family of bandits, once holed up at the King's Head for several days and left with about twelve thousand pounds sterling in stolen property.

Pubs like the King's Head played an active and perhaps overriding role in the social life of the village, where a third of the residences were licensed as alehouses. Few were as fancy as the Conniving House, located just a few yards from the water. An anonymous Brit bunked there for a while, and filed a dispatch full of praise. "Here we used to have the finest fish at all times," he enthused, "and in season, green peas and all the most excellent vegetables. The ale here was always extraordinary, and everything the best. Many a delightful evening I passed in this pretty thatched house with the famous Larry Grogan, who played the bagpipes extremely well; Jack Lattin, matchless on the fiddle and the most agreeable of companions." Acclaimed, too, were the oysters at the Sign of the Good Woman, and the cockles, shrimp, and wine at the Sign of the Highlander.

Though Ringsend lost its currency as a port eventually, it still harbored a fishing fleet and became known as Raytown, because the ships caught so many rays. They caught whiting and mackerel, as well, and also herring to be sold for export, but the fishing declined by the 1850s as did the entire neighborhood, its houses dilapidated and its streets rougher than ever. (In Dublin slang, a "Ringsend uppercut" means a kick in the balls.) Here on

Newbridge Avenue you found the home of the fictional Paddy
Dignam, who died in a drunken stupor and was buried at Glasnevin under the auspices of Mr. Joyce, while Oliver St. John Gogarty, apparently never uninspired, contributed a few celebratory
lines about the village:

> I will live in Ringsend
> With a red-headed whore
> And the fan-light gone in
> Where it lights the hall-door;
> And listen each night
> For her querulous shout
> As at last she streels in
> And the pubs empty out.

It was in Ringsend, too, that Joyce went walking with Nora
Barnacle on June 16, 1904.

With the advent of the dockers, Ringsend flourished again. Beyond the village, Georgian tenements stretched from the Dodder
to Westland Row downtown, where schoolboys finagled tips by
toting the bags of overburdened travelers from the train station
to a taxi or a hotel. In summer the boys swam in the Grand Canal
at Baggot Street Bridge and cavorted among the barrels and
cranes strung along the waterfront, sometimes pulling the bung
from a keg and spilling beer the way kids in Manhattan tap into
fire hydrants, but their mothers played a trickier game by far when
they tried to outwit the rent collector. We'll call him Mr. Wolfe
and extend him some sympathy, because he was terribly over-

matched as the St. Andrew's Heritage Project once recorded in a typical colloquy.

"C'mon, little ladies," Mr. Wolfe might start. "Pay your rent."

"What, I gave it to him, I'm after giving it to you," a mother replies, acting wounded.

"You did not."

She turns to another woman. "Did I not give him the rent?"

"I saw you, sure as God in heaven," the neighbor testifies. "I saw you give him the rent."

"You didn't give me any," Wolfe insists.

"I did give it to you. Now don't stand there and tell me I didn't."

"Oh, hold now, maybe you did. I don't know, I don't remember."

"Well, you better mark it down, because I'm after paying you."

Cowed, Wolfe marks it down, but the mothers aren't done with him yet. Instead, they gang up and accost him in chorus. "I paid you, too," they all swear. "I paid you when she was paying you," and so on until Wolfe admits both utter confusion and absolute defeat, exiting stage left. No doubt Wolfe also heard another standard excuse when he knocked on doors, part of Irish folklore by now, where a child answers and says, "Me mammy inside told me to tell you she was out."

To Willie Murphy, who grew up in a tenement on Holles Street with nine siblings and a docker father, the ruckus would be familiar. As a boy, he earned sixpence a week from a neighbor woman whose husband, a bricklayer, was an awful drunk. When the bricklayer ran through his money, his wife hired Willie to pawn his only suit so she could feed the family, and Willie would pick up the suit again in time for Sunday Mass. (The bricklayer finally fell under a truck and died.) Though his own dad, Willie Sr., drank and gambled, he was still the proverbial good provider and gave Mrs. Murphy fifteen shillings every day, whether or not he had any work. She objected once that Lily down the block got twenty-five shillings, and Willie Sr. agreed to pay that much, but only on the days when he *did* find work. Mrs. Murphy, no gambler herself, backed off and settled for a steady sum.

Willie Murphy told me those stories at his little house off the village hub, as neat and tidy as a ship's cabin. I'd been asking around for someone with roots in Ringsend, preferably a docker who knew the pub scene well, and Willie fit the bill. He was watching an episode of *The Virginian* when I stopped by, Westerns being a staple on Irish TV. He's still a powerful-looking man at the age of sixty-nine, broad through the chest and thick in the forearms, with a standard tattoo on the right one. There was a healthy glow about him, an ease of being. He dressed neatly, too, in jeans, a short-sleeved shirt, and a pair of sandals. His white hair was cut short, and his blue eyes sparkled with wit and intelligence. Though Willie had suffered through the "bad, bad, bad old days," he had an aura of contentment.

Murphys are everywhere in Ringsend, Willie said, patting his dog Charlie. His own family hailed from Wexford, four brothers who labored as sailors and shipwrights and built smacks, or ketch-rigged fishing boats. Willie Sr. followed the usual docker's routine and shaped up before a stevedore every morning for a "read," where the day's jobs were allotted. The men were dispatched to various quays, and those who struck out and failed to be tapped often went right to a pub—one out of every five houses or so, by Willie's count. Even if they were broke, they managed to cadge a drink. They'd hook up with a mate who was "in the goo," solvent rather than "on the slate," in debt to the publican. The cash for pints was never a problem, really. Willie Sr., when short in the pocket, used to borrow a fiver from Billy Lynch, who ran his local, and kept two pounds for himself before he surrendered the balance to his wife.

Dockers were brilliant at funding their habit, according to Willie. They might be employed, but they still signed up for the dole and collected every Tuesday. On Wednesday, they hit the tax office on the chance of a rebate, while on Thursday they received their checks from the Central Pay Office, an obvious cause for celebration. The drinking was every bit as epic as I'd read. The average docker who shoveled coal ate a sandwich and downed two or three pints at the beero hour, and two or three pints before lunch at one, the big meal of the day, and then two or three more during the afternoon break. The serious boozing began after quitting time, when the pubs filled again after the men ate a light supper. The standard measure was six to eight pints, Willie guessed.

"You sweat it out of you in a couple of hours," he swore. "It goes right through you."

"No hangover? No ill effects?"

"Not for me."

The great danger for dockers, it seems, was that they'd spend all their cash on the craic, so they separated the money for household expenses from their drinking stash, tying it up in a handkerchief and tucking it into a shirt pocket. As the evening progressed, the craic affected their judgment, and some fellows dipped into the bundle for another round. At home, the embarrassed offenders avoided their wives and left the expense money, considerably reduced, on a table or a mantlepiece rather than hand it over and risk a confrontation. The wives hated the tactic and sometimes tossed the pittance out a window, shouting, "That's not my money!" meaning it was less than they expected. The dockers reacted with aplomb. "Must be mine, then," they'd say, grabbing the change and reserving it for a pint.

"The women didn't have a look in. It was a fuckin' terrible system in those days." Willie broke into a sly, ironic grin. "The halcyon days of manhood."

Willie joined the system when he left school at twelve and later took a job shoveling coal off the ships. It was filthy, miserable, punishing, sapping work for a young person. Willie's hands were torn up and covered with lumps, callused and bloodied, and the harangues of his bosses were unrelenting. He had no recourse, either. A job of any kind was difficult to land, so you put up with all sorts of abuse. A sixteen-man crew might be ordered to unload 130 tons of coal before the beero hour, driven at an inhuman pace while a crane hovered over them to add to the pressure. If a ship was about to set sail, the crew might be assigned to clear the hold before a specific deadline, and they could be at it until after midnight.

"You'd be a fuckin' wreck," Willie sighed. "It was white slave labor."

After four years of shoveling coal, he'd had enough. He shipped out at nineteen, off to see the world as a steward on an ocean liner. He expected an easy ride, but he was mistaken. Though the job didn't tax him physically, he was on duty from the early morning until nine at night. His supervisors were steely-eyed former officers of the Royal Navy, who monitored his every move and slashed his paycheck for any lapses. He worked the emigrant run to Australia first and has fond memories of the ten-day layovers in Melbourne and Sydney, where the pubs closed at the ungodly hour of six in the evening. To beat the clock, the local dockers drank so much so fast that they passed out on the sidewalk, "worse even than Dublin." Willie's crew couldn't afford the pubs, anyway, so they bought cheap flagons of Penfolds wine.

"Terrible stuff," Willie said merrily, amused by his youthful panache. "I got to drink all over the world."

He made it to South Africa, too, and sailed through the Suez Canal, but he liked New York best of all the ports he visited, because it was so cosmopolitan. He held a staff post on the *Queen Mary* then, a choice assignment, but he thought often of going home. At sea, he underwent a curious transformation. As he put it, "When you travel, you realize your limits." He couldn't abide a future without any promise, so he applied himself on his return to Ireland. While he worked as a salesman, he took classes in business and social studies at night and earned a college equivalency degree. He could feel his horizons expanding, fascinated with the reading for his courses, those fat books on history and biography, the insights packed into them.

He married, as well, and started a family, five children in all. To support them, he worked as a trade union official for twenty-seven years, a post his father had also held for a while. (When the dockers organized a union in 1933, Willie Sr. was a driving force.) Initially, Willie had more than a thousand dockers as members and did a good bit of his canvassing in pubs, but the rolls had dwindled to barely a hundred members by the 1990s due to the mechanization of the port, and a way of life was ending. Still, Willie carried on as he'd always done, hitting his favorite spots and sinking fifteen pints of Guinness every day until the extravagance caught up with him. The doctors checked his liver first—perfectly fine—and next his kidneys—in excellent shape—and took an x-ray of his lungs to see if the coal dust had caused any cancerous lesions, but he passed that test with flying colors, too. His heart turned out to be the culprit, its muscles damaged to the point of near-failure. Willie has been dry since 1998.

"I'll bet you don't even miss it anymore," I said.

"Oh, I do!" he cried, sitting bolt upright. "Jaysus, I do!" At last I'd met a truly heroic pintman, his grip on the glass surrendered only reluctantly.

Willie missed the camaraderie as much as the beer, but whenever he inched into a pub, he listened to his friends and heard absolute rubbish—total nonsense, really, and they went on about it at such length. "Jaysus, that was me," he'd say to himself, relieved to be out of action, although he did succumb once to the illusion that he could drink on the grand scale again. His doctor advised him he could handle two or three pints without any harm, and his hopes soared, yet the doctor meant *per week*. "That would be of no use to me," Willie admitted. "No use at all."

He still felt kindly toward his drinking days, though he understood the toll they had taken. An old pal had just washed up drowned in Dun Laoghaire harbor, in fact—another docker who was *always* in the pub, and the very fellow who had once kicked off a melee at a place called Connor's, when he unlatched the gate of a panel truck parked outside and liberated a flock of geese and turkeys destined for someone's Christmas larder. It was only mid-morning, but the holidays had induced a spirit of revelry. The pints were flowing as if from a fountain, and the men were singing away when into their midst rushed the flapping, gobbling, hysterical birds, knocking over glasses with their wings and throwing a fright into everyone. Willie captured a goose and took it home, where it escaped the usual fate and ended up as a backyard pet rather than on a platter. His wife and children doted on the goose, who even had a pool to splash around in, but it reared up and hissed whenever Willie approached. "Had an awful effect on my sex life," he joked.

That wasn't the case when a docker uncovered a box of amphetamines beneath a tarp on a South African ship, a consignment of drugs being returned to the UK. Somehow the box didn't make it. Instead its contents were parcelled out to Willie and his friends, who'd never taken speed before and were ignorant of its effect—but they quickly learned to like it. Dosing each other became a sport among them, just as hippies used to load the punch with LSD. At the pub you had to take your pint to the gents with you, or somebody would pop in a pill. Nobody could sleep because they were wired all the time, but the women were the beneficiaries for once, treated to nonstop rolls in the hay and puzzled as to why the sex should be so good.

Willie had an agreeable way of unfolding his tales, with a glint in his eye, as if looking back at a foolish—too foolish—and yet courageous younger self, a lad who took his chances, had some fun, and wound up in the clover, but maybe that's how we all regard and even treasure any youthful folly that doesn't end in disaster. The roundhouse right that mercifully misses its target, the silly E-mail sent when tipsy, the one-night stand that results in pure pleasure rather than herpes or worse, they're almost airborne in retrospect, lighter and less threatening versions of themselves, and we shake our heads and decide that it wasn't so bad to have strayed from the straight-and-narrow, after all.

Willie offered to lend me some books about Ringsend as I was leaving, and pulled them from a bedroom closet. A pamphlet from the Watchtower Society of the Jehovah's Witnesses and a flier about the Sacred Heart were stuffed in there, too, and he discarded them with a fair bit of disgust. He'd also stored lots of boating magazines in the closet. "Boats are my second love," he told me. He owns an eighty-foot trawler he once believed he'd convert into a twelve-berth passenger ship for cruises around Ireland and Scotland, but he felt too old for it now. His energy flagged at times, he said, and he got tired. Yet there wasn't a hint of self-pity in his voice. Whatever the outcome, I thought, he'd have few regrets.

The era of the dockers and their gargantuan appetites had guttered out long ago, and one shouldn't be romantic about their pubs, a collection of dives, more or less, modeled on the Flann O'Brien archetype complete with bluebottle flies and yellow sandwich cheese, often dark, dirty, and offensive to the sense of smell. The toilets were an abomination, with floors so wet and slippery with urine that a drunken misstep might lead to a fractured skull, and the smoke was thick enough to induce a coughing fit on entry. If women were admitted at all, they sat in the purdah of snugs, and were ignored or heckled. Sailors often accosted them, although Biddy McGrath gave as good as she got, as a song of the period recounts:

> Now I'll tell you a story that is bound to shock
> It's all about a murder on the Ringsend dock
> I'll tell the story of Biddy McGrath
> Who strangled two sailors with the straps of her bra

> They tried to dope her with foreign liquor
> But even at that they couldn't lick her
> She remembered she was told by her ma and da
> To keep both hands on the straps of her bra

> She put the straps of her bra around the big fella's neck
> And tossed him in the Liffey like a crust of bread
> Then the small fella came up and said, "Hee-Haw"
> So she stuffed his gob with the rest of her bra

Ringsend isn't quite so colorful or dangerous anymore. Its pubs, like so many others in Dublin, try to drum up some business with gimmicks and promotions. Hobblers End hosted Bingo-mania on Monday nights and an evening with the King of Karaoke on Wednesdays. The Oarsman had a Halloween costume party scheduled and live rock every Friday. Sally's Return featured

Texas Hold 'Em and also karaoke, although with no royalty attached. The only entertainment Willie Murphy could remember from his youth was listening to the radio—Flash Gordon and big boxing matches from the U.S. were favorites—and going to the movies if he had the price of a ticket. He gravitated to the pub almost as a reflex, imitating the behavior of his elders. For a young man, the first legal drink amounted to a rite of passage, but hardly anyone engaged in the rite now.

Hobblers End drew me in, anyway, with its nautical associations. A hobbler was a small boat, so called because it rocked back and forth at sea. The skippers, also called hobblers, acted as pilots for schooners and cargo ships, guiding them to port. (The chief cargo was malted barley, destined for the Guinness brewery.) With no way to contact a ship in advance, the skippers raced toward it and used a catching pole to hook it, fighting each other for the reward of a payday. Hobblers were deemed unsafe, though, and banned in 1936, hence their "end." Christy "German" Lawless, the last of the skippers, whose shipmates included Lockjaw, Wee Chucks, Handspike, and Bluenose, lived into his eighties, and his battles with Highwater Flanagan, so grubby he passed as a pirate, haven't been forgotten in Ringsend.

I hoped Hobblers End might have a flavor of the sea, some essence of Melville's Spouter Inn, but it smacked of hotel bars and airport lounges instead, a neutral space that could have been miles from the water. That isn't to say it was unpleasant. The pub was bright, clean, and streamlined, and the owners hadn't scrimped on the furnishings. Food was flying out of the kitchen, an endorsement of the menu, but I still felt oddly detached and switched over to the Yacht, a warmer, friendlier, noisier spot with tons of ship-related ephemera on display, where the regulars clung to their elected perches like barnacles, apparently oblivious (as I was not) of the Elvis and Sinatra videos blaring from a big TV over the front door.

Sally's Return could not be said to beckon. In private, I referred to it as Sally's No Return, because of a scene I'd witnessed outside it, where a man in Paddy Dignam's condition dozed on the sidewalk in bright sunshine. A knot of Ringsenders had gathered to gape at him, among them a schoolboy in uniform about to poke him with a stick to see if he was dead or alive. The Dublin Fire Brigade resolved the issue by sending two paramedics in a yellow ambulance. They donned their sanitary gloves and hoisted the dozer to a sitting position. He opened his eyes and looked shocked to be the center of attention, but since he had no real emergency to address, except perhaps finding the money for his next pint, the paramedics drove off, and he rolled over and went back to sleep.

Sally's made me apprehensive, then, but I bit the bullet and stepped inside. Nobody was asleep on the floor—I suppose I'd been afraid of that. There was nothing to worry about, really. The customers were geriatric men, almost exclusively, and though a few must have been married or widowed, they still constituted a classic example of the bachelors' drinking group, with the pub as their clubhouse and hideout. Some were smartly attired and just making a brief stop on their rounds, while others wore clothes chosen with a haphazard eye and were in for the long haul. The beer cost less than at Hobblers End, and that would matter to pensioners, particularly since many visited Sally's every day. Sally is Sally O'Brien, I learned, who actually did return, having sold the pub in its incarnation as the Shipwright and then bought it back again.

Only the Oarsman remained as a potential oasis of tradition. (The Raytown Bar proved to be an annex of Hobblers End, separated from it by an off-license.) The pub's conversation piece was a massive fieldstone back wall hung with a gilded mirror such as a courtesan might select for her boudoir, and that was a far cry from the ideal. I might have skipped right out if I hadn't recognized Jim, the barman, who used to work at the Waterloo by my twee apartment. He's a softspoken, gentle fellow, and proud to be a consummate professional. You could see it in his clothes. Sharply attired in a black shirt and trousers, he created a favorable impression of order and precision.

"A pint of goodness," he said when he brought my Guinness, a signature remark I recalled from the Waterloo, where he'd been a fixture for more than a decade. Why had he quit? "Me and the woman were after taking over a pub in Longford," he explained, "but the deal fell through." The Oarsman was handy for him, just a short walk from his digs in Ballsbridge down the Dodder path I was so fond of. His usual shift ran from four in the afternoon until closing time, eight hours and a little more. He didn't miss the Waterloo, he told me, because it had changed so much. He had a high opinion of his former boss Christy, who had to contend with the excesses of a "super pub" that could accommodate a huge crowd, but he didn't approve of the new breed of bar staffers, often inexperienced, who glossed over the civilities.

"I mean no disrespect," he continued, adding that race wasn't a factor. His parents had owned a pub in Cavan, so he grew up in the business and was hyperaware of how important a good barman can be in securing the loyalty of customers. (When Paddy O'Brien, a charismatic barman at McDaids during the literary era, tried to buy the pub and lost out to a British woman, he resigned and moved elsewhere. The writers followed him, and their desertion became known as the "flight of the faithful.") A barman needed to interact and chat with people—more than ever now, in Jim's eyes, because a trip to the pub was so expensive. On a night off, Jim might pick up some beer, rent a video, and order Chinese food rather than go to his local, where he could easily spend a hundred dollars, especially if he got coerced into swapping rounds, a practice he disliked.

I agreed with Jim about rounds, of course. Moriarty had taught me the expense—financial, physical, and mental—of the system, but it's been a ritual aspect of Irish pub life for so long that the habit is deeply ingrained. The sociologist Tom Inglis interprets it as an instance of Ireland's "rule-bound society," on a par with the fealty pledged to the church. It's an exercise in social control, Inglis believes, whereas the use of alcohol in most other European countries is much more relaxed and celebratory. Paying for rounds is a way for an individual to gain acceptance—it demonstrates a desire to belong. The system encourages mutual aid and obligation, other critics have speculated, but whatever the case, Jim knew it to be a trap best avoided.

Jim is slender, fit, and usually upbeat, yet he moved stiffly that evening, as hesitant as an old man, and when I asked about it, he revealed that he'd suffered a beating the night before. After he locked up the pub, he started home along the Dodder path, listening to the river and relishing the solitude, when three young drunks approached him from the opposite direction. They jumped him, knocked him to the ground, and kicked him in the ribs, but they didn't rob him. "They were just in it for the craic." He smiled as if to shrug it off, a hand massaging his sore back. "I still hurt everywhere." From now on, he'd call a taxi for safety's sake, and though he wasn't one to moan, it was clear that something *had* been stolen from him—the right to a tranquil stroll along a moonlit river without any threat of harm.

Jim's story haunted me over the next few days. At its core was an image of loss that seemed linked to the decline of the traditional pub and the values it embodies—an accent on community, say, and the bonds required to forge it. You could accuse John Ford of being sentimental and manipulative, but *The Quiet Man* was based on aspects of Irish life that once existed—and still do if you care to believe the Tourist Board's recycled images from the 1950s. In truth, though, the Ireland of the twenty-first century is a very different country, one of the most globalized on earth and suffering through growing pains and an identity crisis, all due to that powdery, transformative dust of change that continues to drift over the island and alter it, for both good and ill.

In the A.T. Kearney Globalization Index for 2007, published in *Foreign Policy*, Ireland ranks fifth behind Singapore, Hong Kong, Switzerland, and the Netherlands. (Ireland was first in 2003, at the height of the Celtic Tiger's clout.) The Kearney index derives its results by a measure of four categories: Political Engagement (foreign aid, treaties, organizations, and peacekeeping); Personal Contact (phone calls, travel, and remittances); Technological Connectivity (the number of Internet users, hosts, and secure servers); and Economic Integration (international trade and foreign direct investment). Like the other leading countries, Ireland is tiny, with a smaller land mass than Indiana. It has no natural resources and a limited domestic market. "When you're a flyweight," the Kearney report states, "globalizing is a matter of necessity."

In some respects, the traditional pub can be seen as a potential victim of the global thrust, since its virtues have always been local and specific. Its gradual disappearance may have an unexplored cultural significance, too, that Perry Share of the Institute of Technology, Sligo, addressed in his paper "Toward an Understanding of the Pub in Contemporary Irish Society." Share found it odd that the pub, so integral to Irish social life, has been studied so infrequently, and he looked to the writings of Ray Oldenburg, an American urban sociologist, to elucidate its importance. Oldenburg came to prominence in the 1990s with his theory of "great good places"—main streets, pubs, cafés, post offices, corner markets, and so on—that are "at the heart of a community's social vitality and the foundation of a functioning democracy."

The great good places are "third places"—not home, the first place, nor work, the second. A third place provides neutral ground that erases the distinction between a host and a guest, impossible at a private party or gathering. It should have a leveling effect, as well, with no criteria for inclusion. Conversation must be the "cardinal and sustaining activity"—not bingo, karaoke, Texas Hold 'Em, or a televised football match. A third place is accessible, ideally on foot, and its success depends on the commitment of its regulars, who build up a network of trust over time. (Students of social capital put a high value on trust, because it's so often violated.) Pubs that operate strictly for profit, or are bought as an investment—faceless pubs, where the publican's an absentee—are less likely to inspire trust than a traditional pub, especially one that's family owned, while super pubs are too big, noisy, and frantic to offer the intimacy necessary for meaningful relationships.

A third place is plain and unpretentious, ordinary and everyday. "The modest décor sets them apart in an image-saturated society," writes Share. (An overly fancy pub, in contrast, calls attention to itself and may lead to restrictive policies at the door.) Being neither home nor work, a third place lets people be playful, unafraid to express themselves, and willing to bend the rules. They get pleasure, says Oldenburg, from "mutually withdrawing from the rest of the world and rejecting the usual norms." And though a third place isn't home, it has some *qualities* of home—a sense of warmth and a freedom-to-be, along with a prospect of regeneration and restoration. Finally, a third place exposes its regulars to novelty, broadens their horizons, invigorates them, and allows them to form and sustain friendships that aren't about "suitability."

"A central aspect of Irish life may be undergoing a significant moment of change," Share concludes, in tacit agreement with Heaney, and my travels so far had done little to dispel that assumption. Change was general all over Ireland, to paraphrase Joyce. Could the traditional pub hold steady in the slipstream of globalization, or would it be swept away? A Starbucks might qualify as a third place, of course, but it would be a *global* third place that could be located anywhere, without any specific, defining, or peculiar characteristics to frank its Irishness. It wouldn't expose its regulars to novelty, nor would it broaden their horizons. There'd be no temptation on the part of the customers, certainly, to reject the usual norms.

Chapter 8

THE COBBLESTONE

To reach Poolbeg Street and the pub called John Mulligan, reputed to serve the best pint of stout in Dublin, you skirt Trinity College and pass a sign on Doyles, another pub, that reads, "There is a good time coming be it ever so faraway." As a believer in omens, I'd have preferred a more blissful one such as, "Deliverance is at hand." After so many wrong turns, I already doubted Mulligan's could live up to its billing. Its Web site named Joyce as a regular—if poor Jim only had a nickel for every bar he supposedly graced!—and I worried I'd once again wind up among some well-intentioned but easily buffaloed tourists. The site showed photos of all the barmen, too, and gave their E-mail addresses in case you wanted to drop a note to Noel, say, and discuss the Sirens episode in *Ulysses*.

Poolbeg Street is a half block from the Liffey, tucked behind some government office buildings. It once led to *Poll Beag*, or little pool, among the deepest anchorages in Dublin harbor. When John Mulligan leased his premises in 1852, moving up from the Liberties as Jack Birchall had done, he competed with two women publicans, a Mrs. McGrath and a Miss McCaul, for business, but he outlasted them. Dockers flocked to his pub, as did traders from the Corn Market on nearby Thomas Street. Actors from the Theatre Royal were also fond of Mulligan's. Judy Garland, Nat King Cole, and Roy Rogers each put in an appearance, and so, too, did such elite members of the racing fraternity as Vincent O'Brien and Mincemeat Joe Griffin, a trainer/owner duo who combined to win the Grand National twice in a row in 1953–54.

Mulligan's looks humdrum from the outside, just a pair of dull yellow storefronts with a brick-fronted lounge bar in between. So little light filtered through the streaked windows I felt as if I'd stumbled into an old country manor only recently opened to the air again after the death of its owner. At a glance, it seemed an honest joint still in its original condition—no recorded music or bric-a-brac, just memorabilia specific to the pub, such as some playbills from Theatre Royal. I recognized the fellow behind the bar from the Web site—Christie, who wore a broad, inviting grin and had the sturdy frame of a baseball catcher.

They say a barman never forgets a face, and I was certain that held true for Christie. (Once I walked into Paddy Cullens in Ballsbridge six months after my first and only visit, and the barman bellowed, "Welcome back!") Christie studied me with an eyebrow arched in amusement, probably because I shifted from foot to foot in a nervous way to keep from blurting out that I knew him, sort of, from the Internet—exactly the kind of ridiculous stab at familiarity a tourist or an innocent would make, and I was neither anymore. Luckily, I repressed the urge and retreated to the lounge, a word that implies a comfort that did not truly exist at Mulligan's.

Instead, my sense of a country manor on the brink of decay was enhanced. The lounge was fairly empty, as if most of the furniture had been sold off to pay the late squire's debts. (James Mulligan, a member of the clan, had banned stools and chairs in his day, because real men should stand up when they drink. The Mulligans' reign ended in 1932.) The walls were a rich rose color and adorned with a half dozen framed etchings, some depicting scenes from Shakespeare's *Henry IV*, an intellectual touch unusual for pubs—maybe Joyce *had* been a regular. If Mulligan's ever resorted to quizzes, you might be asked some trivia about Sir John Falstaff and his buddy Poins. The customers seemed to be boning up for just such an exam, in fact, bent over books and papers except for two lads from Trinity, who were talking about the meaning of life or the desirability of Polish women, or possibly both and how they were interrelated.

I took a seat at a long, hard refectory table. As the seconds ticked by, I was eager to see if the Guinness Christie poured would match its reputation. By accident, through the sheer drudgery of tasting one pint after another all over Dublin, I'd become a semi-expert and approached my stout now with the severity of a veteran sommelier assessing a vintage Chateau d'Yquem. How does the beer look and smell? Has the temperature been monitored properly? Far too often I'd been handed volcanic pints that erupted like Vesuvius and spilled over the rim of the glass, soaking the coaster and causing a sticky situation. There were oddly flavorless pints, too, and pints with a taint of burnt barley, and pints so dreary I almost suspected them of being doctored with dirty dishwater, a practice not unheard-of in earlier centuries.

Guinness was not the only stout on tap, and though I'd tried to escape its hegemony and indulge a lifelong habit of supporting the underdog, I couldn't force myself to switch to Beamish or Murphy's, its chief rivals and both from Cork. (Indeed, Murphy's is difficult to find in the city and difficult to avoid on its home turf.) Beamish is usually the cheapest of the three, but I seldom saw anyone order it and didn't like it when I drank a pint, while Murphy's had more to commend itself, being lighter and more refreshing. Long before Guinness had advertised itself as a boon to health, Murphy's had stolen a march and hired the world-famous bodybuilder Eugen Sandow, born Friedrich Wilhelm Müller in Prussia in 1867, to endorse its product. Renowned for his strongman shows in America, Britain, Ireland, and other parts of Europe, he specialized in bending iron bars and hoisting horses and pianos off the ground.

Sandow wrote a bestselling advice book, *Physical Strength and How to Obtain It* (1897), that turned up in Leopold Bloom's library. The exercises were "designed particularly for commercial men engaged in sedentary occupations," according to Joyce, who had great fun with the book, and "were made with mental concentration in front of a mirror so as to bring into play the various families of muscles and produce successively a pleasant rigidity, a more pleasant relaxation and the most pleasant repristination of juvenile agility." In the Murphy's ad, Sandow lifts a horse and "strongly" recommends his sponsor's stout. When he died at fifty-six while pulling a car from a ditch, an ambitious youth named Alex Kass volunteered to replace him. Kass proposed to hang from a crane and hold a barrel of beer suspended by a wire from his teeth, but the company's directors rejected the stunt as "impracticable."

Time passed slowly at Mulligan's, or maybe it ceased to exist. Somewhere my pint rested, and as I waited for it my mind began to drift. Again I was taken with the sleepy nature of the lounge, its very implacability, and I remembered another Christy, the one J. M. Synge had conjured up in *The Playboy of the Western World*, and how he'd burst into a similarly tranquil pub in County Mayo and startled the regulars by confessing that he'd killed his father. Synge's knowledge of pubs derived in fair measure from his stay on the Aran Islands, where he constantly had to yank his boatmen out of their local.

"With their usual casualness they had not seen to the leak in the curragh," he wrote on one infuriating occasion, "nor to an oar that was losing the toll-pin, and we moved across the sound at an absurd pace . . ." Under the influence of too much porter, the men were "unusually voluble, pointing out things to me that I had already seen, and stopping now and then to make me notice the oily smell of mackerel that was rising from the waves." Even in rough weather, boating accidents were rare on the Arans, Synge learned, and when they did happen alcohol was responsible. Two men, heavy with drink, drowned one day, and their curragh floated to shore "dry and uninjured, the sail half set." Three fishermen from Inishmaan, the second-largest island, also tipped over while drunk, and though a steamer saved two of them, the third perished.

At pubs and in his rented rooms, Synge listened to stories, mostly in Gaelic, and they planted the seed for *Playboy*. One story involved a refugee from Connacht, who fled to Inishmaan, swore he'd killed somebody with a spade while in a passion, and begged his relatives to protect him. He spent weeks hidden in a hole, and nobody revealed his presence despite the offer of a reward. Synge understood that the "impulse to protect the criminal is universal in the west [of Ireland]. It seems partly due to the association between justice and the hated English jurisdiction, but more directly to the primitive feeling of these people, who are never criminals yet always capable of crime, that a man would do no wrong unless he is under the influence of a passion which is as irresponsible as a storm at sea . . . Such a man, they say, will be quiet all the rest of his life, and if you suggest that punishment is needed as an example, they ask, 'Would anyone kill his father if he was able to help it?' "

For Synge, the pub was also a source of revelations, a theme Conor McPherson vamped on in his brilliant play *The Weir*, set in a small rural bar in either Northwest Leitrim (a county blessed or cursed with the most pubs in Ireland) or Sligo. Four gents, testy friends—the publican, a garage owner and his mate, and a real estate agent—tell tales to impress Valerie, a Dublin woman who's just bought a house in the area. The tales are all ghost stories, and each takes the unconscious narrator by surprise, revealing a previously unacknowledged dimension, until the last tale changes the play's direction when Jack, the garage owner, relates a self-lacerating truth that undercuts the earlier evasions. It's the neutral space of the pub as a third place that allows for the confession, which will be left behind when Jack goes out the door. The publican, Brendan, asks, "Will you be okay in that wind?"

JACK. Jaysus, I should be used to that road by now, says you, ha?
BRENDAN. I'll get you the torch.
JACK. Am I a moaner?

BRENDAN (*going*). There's well fucking worse, I'll tell you.

What McPherson captures, as well, is the lingua franca of pubs—the slagging ("to criticize abusively," says the Oxford Concise Dictionary) that some regard as a tactic to puncture any pretension, pierce any inflated egos, and reinforce the democracy of a third place. When Valerie asks for a glass of wine (Jack says, "It's not too often the . . . the . . . wine does be flowing in here."), Brendan goes into his house—the pub is part of the house, common in rural Ireland—to get some. The real estate agent Finbar remarks, "He probably has a bottle of the old vino, from feckin . . . Christmas, ha?" The slagging goes on when the group examines the photo of a dedication ceremony at a weir built to generate hydroelectric power. Finbar singles out a boy in shorts and asks, "Who would you say that is there?"

VALERIE. Is it you?

FINBAR. Would you go ont? The big fucking head on that yoke! Excuse the language. That's Jack.

VALERIE. Oh, my God! How old were you there, Jack?

JACK. Em. Oh I was about seven.

VALERIE. I wouldn't have said that was you.

FINBAR. You must be joking, you'd spot that big mutton head anywhere. The photographer nearly had to ask him to go home, there wasn't going to be room in the picture. Isn't that right Jack?

JACK. That's right, and your dad nearly climbing into the camera there.

FINBAR. He was a pillar of the community, Valerie. No
one had anything against him. Except headers like your
man there. (*Indicating* JACK.)

JACK. That's right, Finbar. And I'm just going in here to do
something up against the pillar of the community now.

All literary thoughts fled when my pint arrived at last. The stout
did not froth, bubble, or threaten to erupt, nor did a ripple run
through it anywhere. Instead it radiated a sense of calm, if such a
thing were possible, and Christie delivered it precisely when the
beer had completed its gyrations and fully settled. The pint was
picture-perfect. A quarter inch of foam topped the black stuff
with its slight ruby tinge, and the stout was cool, not ice-cold,
and crisp and very clean on the palate. Could Christie perform
the same trick twice? I put the challenge to him, and he accepted. His second pint duplicated the first in every detail, a feat
worthy of a citation in, well, *The Guinness Book of World Records*.

My praise was excessive—probably too excessive, to judge by
the ironic look Christie gave me. He'd heard overawed Yanks
spout such nonsense before, I'm sure, but I hung in there and
asked why every pub didn't serve a pint as splendid as Mulligan's.
The duties of a barman aren't as demanding as they once were,
after all. Before Guinness introduced draft stout in sealed aluminum
kegs in 1961, the barmen participated in the weekly bottling car-
nival, when the beer was transferred from barrels into bottles that
needed to be washed, sterilized, and capped. Each pub had its
own label, and it was pasted on by hand. The art of the pint seemed
simple in comparison, so why did it go awry?

"Too many young people," Christie mused. He might have added, "Haste makes waste."

Here was the voice of experience. How many times had a callow lad slaving for the minimum wage brought me an unsatisfactory Guinness? Too many to count, in fact, although you couldn't blame the poor rookie, because he'd never been trained except in the most basic skills. When I checked Mulligan's Web site again, I realized the barmen *were* men in their thirties, forties, and beyond, who cared about the pub, their jobs, and teamwork. Tommy and Con Cusack, the owners, seldom lost or fired an employee, I guessed, but you couldn't go down Ranelagh Road without seeing "Help Wanted" signs in the pub windows, often with the tag "Must Speak Fluent English."

When I next visited Mulligan's, I saw the principle in action. Con Cusack worked the bar with three others, Christie among them, so that made four pint-pullers in all, or double what you'd find in most pubs of the same size, where you have to scramble for a drink as in a rugby scrum. They had no floor staff for support, either, but they weren't rattled and almost seemed geared up to meet and defeat the pressure. In some ways, the pub still reflected the manly attitude James Mulligan had tried to prompt by throwing out the stools and chairs. There'd be no coddling of the patrons, clearly. When your pint was ready, you stepped up to grab it or risked a barman's ire.

Mulligan's by night was a different proposition, though. The manor had come alive. A second bar opposite the lounge, locked during the day, had opened, and it was as crowded as the first. My compatriots from the afternoon before, apart from the Trinity students, were of the gray- and snowy-haired variety, retired or just killing time, but a broad cross-section of Dubliners surrounded me now. There were young office workers from Poolbeg Street, and a good number of dads with teenage sons in tow, who focused on the match between England and Russia that played on two TVs I hadn't noticed last trip.

Tradition or no tradition, it appeared as if television was an unavoidable circumstance of pub life in the modern city. As far as I knew, only the maverick Kavanagh had the nerve to do without one, but maybe he didn't feel the pinch. For most publicans, a big match like England versus Russia, available at home only to those who subscribe to a premium sports channel on cable, provides a welcome shot in the arm. (I heard no rousing cheers for England at Mulligan's, by the way. The Irish have long memories.) As in the U.S., the big breweries buy ad time for these events, and when I looked around the pub, I witnessed a vision of male bonding that replicated to an astonishing degree the carefully staged scenario onscreen.

Soccer bores me, so I bonded with the only other uninterested person at the bar, a German tourist flicking through the pages of *Irland*, his guidebook. He spoke English well, and when I mentioned my California ties, he told me how much he liked the cowboy novels of Karl May. He'd never been to California and placed it next door to Monument Valley, John Ford's old stomping ground—there were some weird coincidental overlaps in the conversation, although I did not, for once, drag in *The Quiet Man*—where, years ago, I'd come across a stack of May novels at a Navajo trading post popular with Germans indulging in Wild

West fantasies. This fellow was very meticulous and had drunk a pint at sixteen of the pubs recommended in *Irland* so far—an excellent country, he agreed, and second only to Germany in its appreciation for beer.

I consulted my two guidebooks later for fun, curious about their take on Mulligan's, if any. *The Rough Guide* repeated the line about the "best Guinness in Dublin," but it touted the pint at the Guinness Storehouse, too. *Lonely Planet* also used the "best Guinness" line, noted that the pub had been a stand-in for Daniel Day-Lewis's local in *My Left Foot*, and commented on the "wonderfully varied collection of regulars." (That would be the daytime bunch, I surmise.) *LP* listed twenty pubs that deserved a visit, not counting twelve "trendy bars" I won't enter in this lifetime, while the *Rough* authors logged thirty-eight pubs to try, leading me to the conclusion that the public house is a vital aspect of Ireland's tourist industry.

The most recent Visitor Attitude Survey (2006) of the Irish Tourist Board offered qualified support for that idea. As usual, The Irish People were the number one attraction, although the admiration for their sociability and all-around charm has been declining steadily for the past five years, perhaps due to the turmoil and edginess that an infusion of new money can create.

Next on the list were The Scenery (inarguable) and Culture/History (somewhat arguable unless you have an insatiable appetite for ruins and castles). If you skip over the next three "attractions" as attributes rather than entities (English Speaking, Access/Easy To Get To, Restful/Relaxing), pubs hold down fourth place, yet most visitors insist they rely on them for food instead of drink, a contention that may require another survey to determine the relative honesty of tourists.

Those visits to Mulligan's gave me a boost. If the pub didn't tick all the boxes, it came awfully close. It might not be as pure as the Gravediggers, but it stuck to the faithful middle ground between the old deadbeat dives of the dockers and such recent aberrations as the new Baggot Inn with its ear-splitting pop music. (In an odd twist, few pubs in Dublin, traditional or otherwise, play recorded Irish music, while the IPC formula practically demands it.) The Baggot Inn has glittering fixtures and promotes its gimmick-of-the-moment, a tabletop device that accepts a credit card and lets you pour your own pint, thereby reducing the contact between people even further. At Paddy Power, you could probably get odds of 5–2 that some young vigilante would soon figure out how to jimmy it and drink for free.

One Saturday afternoon, I walked from Mulligan's to the site of the old Corn Market in the Liberties, only minutes away. *Corn* meant wheat or oats back then, while *maize* was the word for the crop that grows on cobs. It used to be an Irish staple, essential for bread and a valuable export. Account books show that the king's armies in Scotland purchased 113 shipments, each packed in a wicker hamper, in 1229. The market, considerably reduced in size, made its last stand on Thomas Street around 1727, where the traders and farmers reveled at the Bear Tavern and the Hibernian Chophouse. Haberdashers, wool drapers, and purveyors of coarse linens were as prominent as corn merchants, and they hired "pluckers-in," famous for their sheer aggression, to buttonhole pedestrians like barkers and beat them into submission with fantastic promises of bargains never to be met.

The Liberties was buzzing with activity. Even more so than Ringsend, it has the feel of a neighborhood holed up in a bunker to ward off the future. Cranes hover at the edge of it, harbingers of the first high-rises, and tower over the little cottages on Brabazon Square and the statue of Jesus in a gazebo that forms a traffic roundabout nearby. The lure of Grafton Street has no visible impact on the residents, even though the boutiques are just around the corner. Instead, everyone congregates at the junction of Thomas and Meath streets, a free-fire zone of commerce that ought be called Bargainland. Here the discount butchers, bakers, and greengrocers compete with a squadron of open-air vendors, who block the sidewalks with their monumental, vaguely sculptural displays of toilet paper and paper towels in sixteen-piece bundles.

Anyone who's short of money makes a beeline for Cash Converters, where the pawnbroker's three gold balls (a symbol appropriated from the Medici coat of arms) signify a willingness—nay, an eagerness!—to deal. We Loan, We Cash Cheques, We Buy, We Sell, Cash Loans, no financial transaction is beyond the Cash Converters' widely thrown net, and many people choose it over a bank because the formalities are few and don't always require as much documentation. Those who are flush pass it by and upgrade their wardrobes at Bing Bing Fashion or the Bull Ring, an indoor loop of stalls where the selection of track suits, virtually a uniform for the neighborhood youths and some of their parents too, is exceptional.

Amid the hurly-burly, a skinny sad-eyed woman, no doubt a

junkie, tried to sell me some black market cigarettes. Drugs are pervasive on the streets and have led to an epidemic of petty crime. The novelist William Carleton (1784–1869) wrote about the Liberties' criminal element in his autobiography, remembering the night he slept in a "thieves' kitchen" after failing as an apprentice taxidermist—he couldn't stomach the process of stuffing dead birds with potatoes and meal. "The entrance of Dante's Inferno was a paradise compared to it," said Carleton. A host of phony beggars lay on straw mattresses or ragged sheets and drank liquor of every description, while crutches, wooden legs, artificial cancers, scrofulous necks, artificial wens, and sore legs hung from pegs on the walls. Sickened as he might be, Carleton confessed to admiring the thieves' "perverted talent and ingenuity."

Far more noble were the exploits of Robert Emmet, the revolutionary, who was hanged, drawn, and quartered on Thomas Street for his attempt to foment an insurrection in Ireland by seizing Dublin Castle in 1803. The veterans of an earlier rising had promised to send help, and when they failed to deliver, Emmet's men lost their drive, joined the habitual excesses of a Saturday night, and started a drunken mob riot. Armed with muskets and pikes, they inflicted more than fifty casualties. At his public execution, Emmet held a hankie in one hand, obliged to drop it when he was ready. "Not yet," he responded to the hangman's first query, and again "Not yet" to the second, but on the third go-round, he only got as far as "Not—" before the hangman did his duty with apparent zeal, parading around with Emmet's skull in hand and cursing him to the heavens.

Outside St. Catherine's Roman Catholic Church, a white stretch limo pulled up at the curb and released a trio of giggling bridesmaids brilliantly arrayed in pale blue gowns, every inch of them groomed to their own personal ideal of perfection. A gentle mission statement was posted on the church façade ("We are an ordinary people wishing to create a parish where we all feel Welcomed and Valued"), but there'd be nothing ordinary about the wedding ahead. No matter how seriously in hock a family in the Liberties might be, they'll dig deeper to fund a ceremonial bash of any kind—baptisms, christenings, weddings, or wakes—piling on the food, the drink, and extras like a stretch limo and a honeymoon in Bali. Some stores on Thomas Street display basic white "no-frills" communion dresses priced at $500 a whack.

In such an busy, vigorous, integrated neighborhood, the pubs might yet be unspoiled, I thought, but the first three I passed on Meath Street *were* ordinary, no different than an average corner bar in the States. I lingered for a pint at the Fountain, anyway, just to soak up the atmosphere among the shoppers taking a breather in the late afternoon, who were worn out from toting their bags of pork chops, Kerr's Pink spuds, and knobby Brussels sprouts. A trio of TVs each commanded a distinct audience, with the racing fans following the action at Ascot and the soccer fans invested in a Manchester United match. The third TV, mounted high up in a rear alcove, was tuned to a Western for the delectation of two elderly women who ate ham sandwiches, shared a pot of tea, and speculated about whether Randolph Scott was really gay.

Two bruisers caught my eye, older men with a long history of hard physical labor etched into their faces. They resembled figures from the past, out of step with the present and glad of it, one with a bottle of Mackeson's Triple Stout—a first in my experience—and the other sipping a vodka and Finches Lemonade. They fell silent when I approached the bar. Strangers don't wander into the Fountain very often, so a newcomer bears examining. The scrutiny, though harmless, still caused me to twitch, and I half expected them to mutter a derogatory comment and maybe upbraid me for nosing around where I didn't belong.

Quite the opposite happened, though. The young barman, green and inept, ignored me to watch the soccer match, so the larger and more leonine bruiser banged a fist on the bar—*kapow!*—and nodded in my direction. The lad's cheeks burned, and he leaped to attention, as if the fist had struck him on the head. The bruiser's gesture on my behalf, so polite and aware, had less to do with my discomfort, I believe, than with a desire to uphold the dignity of the Liberties, his home turf, and show it in the best possible light. *It's not as tough as you've heard, stranger*, he might have said. He accepted my thanks, but he refused the offer of another vodka, since he felt no need to be repaid for a simple good deed.

Sunday once constituted the big day for Irish pubs, a festival that began right after Mass and could continue for hours. The hungover gents who'd survived the service, often with heads as inflated as beachballs, were the first in line for a barstool, but there were also couples whose only visit of the week occurred after church, more for the society than the alcohol. In some households, the rib roast or leg of lamb due to be carved for lunch at two o'clock rested on a sideboard until five or six, when a child might be dispatched to collect the paterfamilias. Because St. Catherine's was such a focal point in the Liberties, I returned to see if the ritual might still have some currency, but the folks in the pubs appeared to be the same ones who had closed them down the night before, at least to judge by the absence of finery and the mild aura of woe.

Fortunately, I had a backup plan. A friend had advised me that if I wanted to hear a real session of traditional music, I should hike over to the Cobblestone across the Liffey, where the Sunday afternoons are special. The route I followed took me by Christ Church and past the Brazen Head, once again thronged with tourists. I didn't intend to stop, but curiosity got the better of me, and I saw that music was the draw here, too, although in a much more informal setting than on my last trip. The musicians sat at a corner table near the bar—no stage, no microphones, and no patter. They were pros, but they seemed relaxed and in no hurry to please. They had the look of contented, road-weary trouba-dours, who were glad to have an audience and yet might have been just as happy playing to an empty room.

Their music—guitar, fiddle, bodhran, and bones—was much less folksy, too, and might have sounded the same fifty or a hun-dred years ago. It was so fast, furious, and irresistible that I had a problem with my left foot: it wouldn't quit tapping. Perhaps that wasn't so odd, since the tunes were originally created to accom-pany the jigs, reels, and hornpipes that itinerant dancing masters once taught from village to village, often with a blind fiddler as a partner. (Smallpox usually caused the blindness, and the afflicted took up the fiddle.) When I left after an hour, I felt satisfied rather than diminished. The Brazen Head had redeemed itself for the time being. Any trophy pub that's a tourist haven probably de-serves a medal for getting it right even half the time.

The Cobblestone is located on the edge of Smithfield Market, a cobbled square that's described, in long-winded terms, as the "largest purpose-built open civic space in Europe." Cattle were first sold there in 1541, driven in from farms in County Meath and herded through Oxmantown Green. The cattle were gone by 1665, and the market gradually diversified and still housed some wholesale dealers of fruit and vegetables when I first settled in Dublin. They're gone now, banished in the throes of a massive redevelopment project that has turned the square into a patchwork of apartments, office blocks, and stores with such corporate anchors as a Comfort Inn, a Subway "restaurant," and a Thomas Read pub. Smithfield belongs to the new city of glass and steel, not the old one of bricks and mortar, but it regains a bit of soul when the horse fair, a centuries-old tradition, occurs on the first Sunday of every month.

I'd attended the fair and can testify that the horses will never run at the Curragh, Ireland's premier racetrack, or anywhere else, not when you can pick up one for three hundred dollars or so. You might be better off buying a donkey or a ragged, piebald pony such as those that are prized by a subculture of teenage boys who live on the outskirts of Dublin, often in stacks of subsidized flats with some open space around them. They're disadvantaged kids, but they manage to scrape together enough money to swap it for a nag of their own. The pony might pull a trap some day, but the boys prefer to show off and ride it bareback, dressed in their hoodies, jeans, and sneakers over roads where it shouldn't go, adopting it as a status symbol and an emblem of their bravery, although their boldness gets them into trouble if they veer too close to a highway.

Long ago, the turfmen from the bogs of Kildare took a similar risk when they brought their peat to Smithfield. First they canvassed the adjoining streets, crying "Turf! Turf!" and selling clamps of it for tuppence a dozen. They also sold bundled twigs to light a fire, and when they were done, they might steal a nap on the cobbles beneath their cart. They often spent their profits on ale and whiskey, so a turfman, drunk and asleep, was frequently spied trotting home along the Lucan Road and counting on his horse to know the way. Trams were a danger, and so many turfmen were killed near a pub in Palmerstown that it acquired the nickname of Deadman Murphy's.

At an average Smithfield fair, there may be fifty horses for sale, paraded around by the bridle and depositing steamy piles of manure, while the potential buyers pry open a mouth to inspect the stubby brown teeth or kneel to poke a suspicious hock. Pony boys are on the prowl, ready to trade their current mount for a new one, if only for the hell of it. Travelers are present, too— members of the gypsy tribe formerly called tinkers, who once crossed Ireland in caravans and worked as tinsmiths and peddlers, fortune tellers and entertainers, confidence artists and farmhands. They conversed in shelta, a language "concocted for the purposes of secrecy," as one linguist has put it, "by a community living in the midst of Irish speakers." Horses were important to them, so they bred the Irish cob, stocky and powerful, with a kindly disposition, to pull their wagons.

Alcohol complicates the lives of travelers. They're often barred from pubs, even though it's illegal. Drink makes them feisty, the argument goes, and brings out a violent streak that leads to brawls and worse. The violence is seldom directed at outsiders. Instead it erupts as the result of a smoldering feud. Travelers can be clannish and slow to forgive or forget an insult or an imagined slight. At times, they throw huge wedding celebrations that are even more elaborate and expensive than the shindigs in the Liberties, and invite anyone even remotely acquainted with the bride or the groom. The receptions can be incendiary, because of the quantity of booze consumed. A bash at Tinakilly House, an elegant hotel in Wicklow, had generated fodder for the tabloids not long ago, in fact, when two warring factions attacked each other with machetes, axes, slash-hooks, knives, and shotguns, much to the consternation of the paying guests.

The Cobblestone turned out to be plain and unaffected, deliberately so, as if to thumb its nose at the Comfort Inn and the Subway. Inside, I found a diverse crowd—young and old, men and women—perched around a cushioned nook by the front door, where some players were seated and tuning up. The walls of the downstairs bar are lined with posters for gigs and photos of musicians, some famous and some not, and there's also an upstairs lounge where you can hear a different type of music every night—folk rock, flamenco, jazz, and so on. Much to my delight, the Cobblestone doesn't have a TV. Moreover, the Sunday session is free of charge.

I took a stool at the bar, ten feet away from the players. They were a mirror image of the crowd, mixed in terms of their age and sex—Jan on the uillean pipes; Dan on the mandola, bigger than a mandolin and related to the lute; Deidre on the fiddle; and Mick on the flute. Also sitting in, sort of, was Aisling, Deidre's daughter, whose fingers flew over the controls of a Nintendo Game Boy, as if to coax some companionable notes from it. The players did not work together professionally, and may never have met before for all I knew. Insofar as they had a leader, it was probably Mick by virtue of his seniority. Benign and grandfatherly, he wore a tie and a maroon cardigan, and established a mood of respectful decorum.

Though Mick sometimes launched a tune, he chose not to dominate the group. Anyone could begin with a bar or two, and the others would join in or remain silent. The piper gave many tunes a pass. Every tune was improvised and more spirited because of it, reeled off at a fever pitch and rich in unexpected twists and discoveries, with the players bouncing off one another and coming at it from new angles rather than sticking to the old ones—*exploratory*, that was the word for it. The sound was fresh instead of canned, full of juice instead of sucked dry.

Sitting so close, I could feel an invisible barrier that the players created around themselves, as if to protect the magic. Their pace was leisurely, not forced. They had no set list or time limitations. They were communing with the eternal. They broke for long, meditative pauses between tunes, talking amiably and content to wait for inspiration to spark the next move, and then someone would strike a chord in the same way that a person clears his throat, and the fever was on them again. I was surprised by the music's power. The emotion welled up out of nowhere, it seemed, and caught me unawares. The music came to me as a gift, and it nourished me. There was no question of longing for Ireland, or pining for Glocca Morra. I knew myself to be in the presence of the genuine, absolutely rooted in it.

I'd have been grateful enough for that, but the Cobblestone had more in store. A darkly handsome young man—jet-black hair, a cleft chin, flashing eyes, every inch the cinematic image of a wandering minstrel—emerged from the rear of the bar and asked

Mick if he could sit in. He felt poorly, he confided, because two pals had "kidnapped" him and hauled him from pub to pub for the past week, capping their adventure by polishing off a case of beer, or twenty-four half-quart cans, the night before. "I'd say that's a friendship you can't afford," Jan, the piper, joked, and the youth—we'll call him Derek—grinned ruefully and replied, "The cash is gettin' low." He ordered a Guinness at the bar and mumbled, "Hair of the dog," and then emptied the coins from his pockets, put them in stacks by denomination, counted them, and pushed across the required sum, only to be rebuffed by Tom Mulligan, the pub's owner, who happened to be tending bar and wouldn't let him pay.

Derek carried a battered case, and unlatched it to reveal a red accordion. It was more compact than the bulky version forever associated in my mind with Lawrence Welk and polka bands, so I mistook it for a concertina and later breached the etiquette of the session by asking him about it. "Accordion," he snapped at me. "Button, not piano." Traditional musicians bridle at such queries, apparently, because it interrupts the flow. They're superstitious about their instruments, too, and only think of themselves as custodians. After my faux pas, Derek gave the red accordion a squeeze and—without any signal to the others—plunged into a tune. His passion and dexterity were more fuel for the blaze, so the level of intensity increased, and the players grew more frenzied. Derek's music had the black sounds in it. It had *duende*. The music was a cure to him, a healing balm. It blew away the cobwebs of his hangover and restored his vigor.

So it went through the afternoon, but the session drew no attention to itself. Some customers stayed close by and listened, but others talked quietly and treated the music as a backdrop. Two more players came along after a while, a father and his teenage daughter, who was a little older than Aisling and in the first full flush of adolescence, with braces on her teeth and a fiddle case under her arm. As she applied some rosin to her bow, her dad unpacked a set of pipes, and though the girl was not in the same league as the others, even squeakily discordant on occasion, they still welcomed her to their company and urged her on. In the warmth of the gesture, there was an implicit understanding of time and patience as traditional music's only teachers.

The genial Tom Mulligan presided over it all, never collecting a dime from the players for stout or tea. Affixed to his lips was a permanent smile of delight, as if the good vibrations had surpassed his desire to supply them. Mulligan had bought the Cobblestone in 1987 for about $125,000, when the pubs in rundown Smithfield were the city's cheapest. It was "an early house with four dartboards and plenty of odd characters behaving even odder," he once said, but it's worth millions now. Still, Mulligan thought the Cobblestone lived on borrowed time, operating under a preservation order due to its historical status. "It'll be a sad day for the inner city and cultural Dublin when it is pulled down." Like the horse fair, soon to be relocated to a vacant lot far from Smithfield, the pub would give way to more glass and steel.

Chapter 9

THE FOLLY OF CONG

M Y ATTENTION TURNED to rural pubs that autumn when Charles Crockatt, a Ranelagh friend, invited me to visit his cottage in County Sligo for a couple of days. As a Birchall's regular, Charles is a knowledgeable man with a jar, so I didn't have to twist his arm to get him to agree to show me the locals near his spread. The plight of such pubs was in the news again due to the advocacy efforts of Paul Stevenson, who heads up the Vintners Federation of Ireland, a trade organization. More than a thousand of its members, all in the country, had closed in the past three years, Stevenson alerted the press. "There isn't enough business—simple as that," he said, laying the blame on a number of familiar factors including "lifestyle changes." Publicans needed to diversify and adapt, he added, and as an example he suggested they could operate as an Internet café until the drinkers arrived at night. Even to an optimist, that sounded improbably far-fetched.

Sligo is known and promoted as Yeats Country, of course, where the great man's remains lie in the churchyard at Drumcliff in the shadow of Benbulben. As I packed my bag, I recalled how little affection Yeats had for pubs and imagined that he might not be disturbed by their decline. Only once did he stoop to enter a licensed premises, dragged into James Toner on Lower Baggot Street by the insistent St. John Gogarty, where he hid in a snug and sipped a sherry. "I have seen a pub," he sniffed as he finished his drink. "Will you kindly take me home?" That hadn't prevented Toner's from slapping a portrait of Yeats on an outside wall, seated next to the poor, overworked James Joyce, and claiming him as a regular.

It's about a three-hour trip from Dublin to Sligo if you're not caught behind a tractor or a big rig, but I hadn't been on the road for more than an hour and a half before the pub crisis crossed my radar in the hamlet of Annaduff, just beyond the village of Dromod. I pulled over to buy a soda at a shop next to Top o' the Hill, a pub on the highest ground for miles around, with views over green fields that could have earned a Tourist Board seal of approval. When I asked the clerk at the shop how Top o' the Hill was doing, she replied, "Terrible!" It only opened at night to serve a few pensioners, who live nearby and can reach it on foot. The stiff penalties for driving while legally drunk had scared away most other customers. For a borderline offense, you lost your license for at least three months. If you failed a breath or a urine test, you couldn't drive for at least two years, a serious hardship out in the country where a car is essential.

These strict laws are relatively new in Ireland. When the government tackled the problem in the 1990s, for instance, it coined the slogan, "Just two will do." In other words, two pints was a permissible measure for a driver, especially given the practice of rounds, but there have been so many horrific accidents on the back roads—the Republic has never had so many cars, nor so many people handling them recklessly—that some action had to be taken. The back roads, often isolated two-lane blacktops with no streetlights, now carry fifteen times (my guess) the traffic they once did as the number of commuters grows by leaps and bounds. That growth had altered Dromod beyond recognition. "It used to be a lovely little village," the shopwoman sighed, but a farmer had sold off one of those lush green fields a while ago, and a row of cookie-cutter houses, the area's first surburban tract, soon replaced the sheep and the cows.

All along the N4 highway to Sligo, I saw similar tracts of houses devouring the land that had been farmed for centuries. In Carrick-on-Shannon, the city center had almost disappeared in a welter of construction. I remembered Dessie Hynes's idyllic description of smoking reeds on the banks of the river, and also an article I'd read by John Gormley, a leader of the Green Party and the current minister for the environment. A native of Limerick, he'd played along the Shannon as a boy, too, when the water was clear, clean, and safe for swimming, but the river is poisoned and dead near his childhood home now, polluted by industrial, domestic, and agricultural effluents. That shocked Gormley. Pollution happened in other countries, he said, while Ireland was supposed to be a "very beautiful, kindly, and spiritual place."

Sligo lies in the province of Connacht, famous for its poor soil and its link to Oliver Cromwell, and as a bastion of the Anglo-Irish Ascendancy that made life a misery for Catholics in the eighteenth century. The scale of the discrimination was astonishing. A Catholic couldn't sit in the parliament, or be a solicitor, a gamekeeper, or a constable. They weren't allowed to attend university, either in Ireland or abroad, nor could they keep a school. Instead, they relied on "hedge schools," where itinerant teachers lectured students in the open air. Priests said Mass in secret, too, at rocks and sites known only to the faithful. A Catholic orphan had to be raised as a Protestant, while no Catholic could own property or receive it as a gift.

Today, Sligo has about eighteen thousand residents, the largest city in the northwest. With its concentration of restaurants, clubs, theaters, and so on, it resembles a miniature Dublin, and its pubs, nearly fifty of them, must compete just as fiercely for business. Agriculture still contributes to the economy, but not in the same dominant way it once did. After you creep through the downtown streets and cross over the Garavogue River, you've entered Yeats Country proper. (I passed a sign for Oliver Goldsmith Country on the N4, but nobody was rushing toward Longford. *She Stoops to Conquer* lacks the panache of Innisfree.) The sky seems to expand, the air tastes fresher, and the poet's beloved Benbulben looms ahead, a magnificent table mountain composed of limestone and shale, with jagged outcrops that catch the light or vanish in shade as the clouds sail by.

When Yeats died on the French Riviera in 1939, he was buried in Roquebrune-Cap-Martin, but he instructed his wife George to "plant" him in Sligo after the newspapers had forgotten him, and he was reinterred at Drumcliff a decade later. Tour buses jam the churchyard's parking lot in summer, but the high season was over, so I had the grounds mostly to myself. As I kicked through piles of leaves and heard the wind whistle along the face of Benbulben, I recited some favorite lines and also remembered, weirdly, the Cranberries' "Yeat's [*sic*] Grave." "Sad that Maud Gonne couldn't stay," they sang, "but she had MacBride anyway." The sacred mingled with the profane at Drumcliff—in my mind, anyway—but that probably wouldn't have bothered Yeats. After he underwent the Steinach operation, a form of vasectomy (no monkey glands involved), at the age of sixty-nine, he began a raging affair with Margot Ruddock, a poet, singer, and actress, and even snuck some of her work into the *Oxford Book of Modern Verse* as its editor.

Inevitably, a Yeats Country Tavern lay just down the road, and I later noticed his name slapped onto other bars, hotels, and gift shops to create an utterly prosaic anti-poetry that would have been even more offensive if it hadn't been so predictable. The shameless exploitation of dead Irish writers for commercial purposes was a national scandal, really, when you consider that most visitors had never read a word they put to paper. (The natives *have* to read a few words, at least, to pass their school exams.) I was glad to leave the morass and turn onto the road to Lissadell, my destination, formerly the ancestral home of the Gore-Booths, whose daughters Eva and Constance were intimates of the young Yeats. He appears to have lusted after them, as evidenced by his poem "In Memory of Eva Gore-Booth and Con Markievicz." Con, the more rebellious, had married and divorced a Polish count, and was a hero of the Easter Rising.

> The light of evening, Lissadell,
> Great windows open to the south,
> Two girls in kimonos, both
> Beautiful, one a gazelle.

I drove through little Carney, where the two pubs had not yet opened their doors and another new tract of houses looked down on them from a hillside. Rounding toward Lissadell, I caught glimpses of the Atlantic, and October sunshine on biscuit-colored beaches. More leaves in their autumn glory swirled and danced. When the Gore-Booths sold their estate in 2003, Charles Crockatt had the foresight and the nerve to buy a two-acre parcel with a derelict cottage that would have terrified a lesser fellow. Charles is a capable type, though, and he's blessed with a pioneer spirit and a can-do attitude. The cottage needed everything from a roof to new plumbing and wiring, but he made it habitable and then comfortable, and now he hoped to finish a two-bedroom extension before Christmas, doing most of the work himself.

I found Charles in the kitchen when I arrived. He's a wiry, athletic man, and he hovered over the stove, a reconditioned Aga, covered in plaster dust and cooking the kind of hearty lunch a worker deserves—a bacon sandwich on a baguette and some eggs baked in ramekins, followed by a cup of tea and a roll-up smoke from a pouch of Sweet Afton. Though Charles is a builder by trade, his enthusiasms are a better clue to his personality—bridge, tango, cricket, and yoga, I am consistently dazzled by his enlightened energies while I nod off over a book. Born in England, he migrated to Ireland in his youth and never looked back, marrying an Irish woman and starting a family. The country suits him, he says, and he seems to take a certain ease in the distance from his roots, a common attitude among expats.

When Charles and I meet at Birchall's for a drink, I adjust my schedule to his, since he favors the Irish pattern of going for a pint after dinner while I am a captive of the American cocktail hour, and we'd do the same tonight. There were three pubs within a five-mile radius of the cottage, each a stand-alone with no village or businesses nearby, and hence as rural as can be. It was possible that they might not all be open, Charles warned, because the publicans were whimsical about the hours they keep. Closing time is particularly fluid, and a "lock-in" to facilitate after-hours imbibing is a practice with a long, intrepid history. Also, the pubs were all part of the owners' houses, just as in McPherson's *The Weir*.

After lunch, Charles returned to his labors, so I thought I'd drive out to the ocean for a walk on the beach, but I got waylaid at a crossroads where a white house advertised itself as McLeans, both a shop and a pub. McLeans opened at four if you believed a note on the front door, but it was already four fifteen and the door was still locked, confirming the advance intelligence I'd received. I sat at a picnic table outside to wait, and watched two donkeys slowly strip the grass from an adjacent field, an oddly engaging spectacle. A cat mewled in a brilliantly Barbie-pink house on the opposite corner, but the silence of the countryside was otherwise imperturbable, broken only by the noise of an occasional car.

At four thirty, McLeans opened at last. The shop was the size of a shoebox and stocked with the staples of a convenience store. A door separated it from the pub, where I instantly established myself as the only customer and introduced myself to Helen McLean, an attractive woman of sixty, who'd been pulling pints for thirty-seven years. Her private life was secured behind another door that led into the house she shared with her husband Hugh. They had raised three sons together—the donkeys, Harry and Fred, had been the boys' pets—but the boys were grown men now and all certified public accountants in Dublin, who only come back to Ballyscannel—the name of the crossroads—on weekends and have no interest in taking over when their parents retire, a tune I'd heard before.

Hugh's family had started the business. He joined us from time to time, shuttling between the shop and the pub, a trim, easygoing man with a hint of the accountant about him, too, that sense of accuracy and stability. He joked about the old farmers he had known as a child, who actually did smoke clay pipes and spit on the floor, whether or not any sawdust was spread to assist with the cleanup. The farmer Roddy Feehily came by horse and cart, and swore that the horse halted at McLeans of its own volition, refusing to move until its master had a drink. Ballyscannel was strictly a farm community then, but only two big farms were left. The livestock I'd seen belonged to hobbyists, Hugh told me, and they had jobs in Sligo and were commuters like those in Dromod.

The pub hadn't changed much since its inception. Hugh touches it up every couple of years, but only for cosmetic reasons. If two football teams chose to shake hands over some beer after a game, they couldn't fit inside. There are five stools at the bar and three tables to the rear, although nobody ever sits at them, even when the stools are taken. The regulars at McLeans are as hidebound and stubborn as all the rest, and they treat those tables as they might a spell in jail. Helen had spruced up the area with a photo of a Grand National winner scaling Beecher's Brook, a tricky fence at Aintree Racecourse in Liverpool, that she'd inherited from an uncle who owned the horse, but it did no good. The men—most regulars are men—stayed put.

Helen comes from Ballina on the River Moy in Mayo—the Irish give the "o" a lilt—and she'd met Hugh when she moved in with a sister in Sligo and took an office job. They used to go ballroom dancing in Bundoran, a seaside resort in Donegal, and she remembers the outings fondly. Ballyscannel in those days was still a village. Every Friday, a "traveling bank" dropped by the cross-roads to distribute pension checks and other handouts from the government, and McLeans could barely cope with the overflow. The pub has no such windfalls at present, Hugh assured me, and yet his business was still quite decent. He earned more from the pub than the shop, in fact.

That surprised me, since I expected a sob story to corroborate the statistics Paul Stevenson had trotted out. Hugh was sanguine for the moment, though, and maybe lucky. The drink-driving laws hadn't undercut his trade, because the local police were be-ing judicious. Only two officers were stationed at Grange, about ten miles away, and they could identify almost every car parked at McLeans and knew pretty much everything about the drivers. Hugh also counted on the loyalty of his customers, some of whom were old pals from high school and couldn't live without the gossip. The newcomers to Ballyscannel didn't have such deep ties to the community, so they used the pub less frequently.

The first regular doddered into the pub around six o'clock, an elderly Brit in a tweed coat and cable-knit sweater, who looked every bit the country gent and needed only a sheepdog trailing him to complete the illusion. He asked Helen for a bottle of alcohol-free Beck's beer and poured it over ice—many of the Irish do the same with their lager and cider—and unfolded the latest edition of the weekly *Sligo Champion*, a paper he'd once written for, and flipped through the pages. I tried to strike up a conversation, but his hearing aids were on the blink. He'd plunked them on the bar next to his beer bottle, but he did admit he loved Ballyscannel. The only way he'd ever leave, he said, was in a coffin.

The sight of the *Champion* reminded Helen of an anecdote about a Canadian neighbor, who lit out for Ireland after his marriage fizzled. He grabbed a bundle of papers in Dublin and liked what he read about Sligo, so he toured the county and wound up in Ballyscannel by chance, where he bought a house. Helen and Hugh seemed to agree that the Canadian had been very fortunate, indeed, and that the charms of their little chunk of paradise couldn't be overstated. They had no desire to see America and its treasures. Hugh's one trip to the U.S.—to Orlando, Florida—had satisfied that urge forever, although Paris still appealed. Instead of a steady diet of travel, the McLeans had other plans for their golden years. When they sold the business, they intended to build a new house in a field three hundred yards away.

Charles Crockatt is a creature of habit. He takes a measured, methodical approach to life and indulges in a hot bath when he completes his daily chores. Suffice it to say that he was very clean when he emerged from the steam and vapors, ready to guide us on a spin through the hinterlands. For ballast, we ate a dinner of strip loin steaks, Sligo spuds, and cabbage, after which Charles, who has a sweet tooth, dug into a berry pie. His metabolism allows him to exercise a cavalier disregard for calories, and he will even brag to you about his resting pulse rate if you let him. Our first stop would be Ellen's, he told me, since I'd already been to McLeans on my own. Ellen's had lots of, or possibly too much, character, and we'd go on from there to Jordans for our nightcap.

We departed at nine thirty. The night was black and starless, with the mercury dropping toward freezing. Somewhat reluctantly, I agreed to drive, feeling obligated as the guest. The side roads, dangerous by day, could be lethal after dark, particularly for a stranger. They were no more isolated than usual, just too narrow. Two cars could squeeze by each other if neither driver panicked or suffered a drug-induced hallucination, but the shoulder as such didn't exist at some junctions, and an informal game of chicken ensued. You backed up or your opponent did, and if you were the chicken, you prayed that no stoned kid in a fast car was approaching from behind—boy racers, Charles called them. Tall hedgerows lined the road on both sides at times, as well, blocking your peripheral vision, and you felt as if you were barreling blindly down a tunnel to oblivion.

I proceeded gingerly, on the lookout for the police I was now convinced would arrest me even before I sipped the froth off a pint. I began to relax after about ten minutes, though, when I realized we hadn't seen another car since leaving the cottage. My anxiety about the coppers subsided, too. It would take a dedicated officer to patrol the wilderness we were negotiating. Besides, the roads discouraged any automotive bravado unless you were a boy racer. On a cold night, with a threat of frost in the air, the two guys in Grange were more likely to sit by a warm stove and enjoy a cup of coffee rather than set up a checkpoint in— well, I didn't have a clue where we were.

Sadly, Charles was also baffled. "It's the next right, or the one after that," he guessed, a literal stab in the dark, and my anxiety returned with a vengeance. There were no signs for Ellen's, of course, nor for any towns, but that wouldn't have helped since

Ellen's wasn't *in* a town. It was merely a pinprick of light in those otherwise vast black fields, and whether or not we'd ever locate it was a logical question to ask. I turned right, I turned left, and then I turned around. The roads all looked the same to me, and we surely traversed the same one twice. I almost wished for a policeman now, if only to ask for directions. Even Charles's confidence had faltered, and he was making the first tentative steps toward admitting that we might be lost.

Yet our salvation lay just around the next bend. Again the road looked identical to all the others, but Charles felt certain he'd nailed it at last. He sat forward in excitement, an arm extended in the manner of an explorer on the brink of a grand discovery—the source of the Nile, say—and pointed to the pinprick of light we were seeking. Ellen's! We were both thrilled, and almost celebrated with some high fives. Like McLeans, Ellen's was an ordinary house, but not as inviting. Rather than being bright and cheerful, it had a dour aspect and did little to disguise its primary function as a residence. It could have been a frontier outpost hunkered down in the face of hostile forces.

Ellen's was unique, all right, and appeared to be oblivious of the need to attract any customers—shebeen-like, really. There was a slight element of trespass when we entered, accentuated by the dim and gloomy lighting. It occurred to me that Ellen (if there was one) might be asleep somewhere, and I actually began to tip-toe for a few seconds until I came to my senses. Again I thought of *The Weir*. The pub was spooky enough to act as a set for the play, with the ghost stories flying. We passed through a small bar, where a TV once again blathered to an audience of vacant stools, and into the Long Hall, an underfurnished room spacious enough for a barn dance. Its centerpiece was a pool table, with a dartboard as backup. Only ghosts were shooting eight-ball, though, or aiming for the bull's-eye.

A chill cycled through the Long Hall, so we gravitated toward a stone fireplace where logs were blazing. A merry gent sat beside it, his cheeks flushed from the heat and as red as a Delicious apple, and he raised a hand to greet us like long-lost pals, but he may just have been lonely and hoping for some company. At ten thirty, Ellen's had only three other stalwarts in attendance, each in solitary contemplation of his jar. Their mood was desultory, as if a night at the pub was a dreary job they meant to quit as soon as they could. Charles was puzzled. Ellen's must have fallen on hard times, he reckoned, or endured a serious deprivation of the randomly distributed craic. In balmier days, folks from Sligo had crowded the place after a drive to the beach, but maybe they were too intimidated now and worried they'd have to evade a dragnet to avoid being collared.

After my talk with the McLeans, I couldn't tell how much of this was paranoia and how much a legitimate fear. Top o' the Hill, on a busy highway, might be subject to constant scrutiny, but I doubted the patrol from Grange staked out Ellen's very often. If they did, they could probably make arrests to their heart's delight, and the same would be true at every other pub. Still, the myth of ceaseless surveillance had incredible power. Even some clergymen were scared of being apprehended, however accidentally. If a country priest conducted more than one Mass on a Sunday, shuttling between parishes, he might drink enough communion wine to be legally incapacitated, advised Father Brian d'Arcy of Enniskillen.

Some publicans grumbled that the whole situation smacked of hypocrisy. The cops were scarcely perfect human beings, after all. Edna O'Brien once told of a high-ranking officer on an inspection tour of County Clare, who visited a station in Corofin where his men had drunk all the kegs of poteen they'd confiscated from a bootlegger. When the desk sergeant rose to salute his superior, he toppled into a fireplace. The men had also cuffed three innocent women and compelled them to join the party, later locking them in a cell. As the officer left in disgust, he encountered the besotted sergeant again. "He started to argue with me on the footpath, with his private parts exposed," the officer noted in his report. "Each syllable was punctuated by bursts of urine against the road."

Charles and I gradually warmed to Ellen's. It might not be the liveliest pub around, although it could be if the craic deigned to return someday, but it still had a rustic appeal. The owners emerged from their quarters to chat with the three stalwarts, who became more animated, as if the attention had awakened them from a deep slumber, while we shot some pool and listened to the clatter of the balls echo through the Long Hall. The merry gent grew merrier and more flushed. We had wasted so much time during our period of being semi-lost that Charles deemed it unwise to carry out a second search for Jordans—though he knew *exactly* where it was—so we settled for a last pint at McLeans where, sure enough, about ten regulars gathered around the five barstools and shunned the tables at the rear.

Of all the ill-advised decisions in my life, the one I made the next morning qualifies as the topper. Charles began to hammer floorboards after breakfast, perfectly content to have me idle by the

Aga or take the beach walk I had postponed the day before, and later escort me to Jordans as planned, but I happened to glance at my map and notice that Cong was only about two hours away on the road to Galway—a good road, Charles assured me, where I'd experience no squeeze factor or involuntary games of chicken. Simply put, I couldn't resist a look at the pub that the Quiet Man Movie Club had shipped over from Hollywood. My innocence had returned with a vengeance, and the romance of Ireland had me in its clutches once more.

The Galway road was wet and slippery after the frost, and a thick fog hung in the hollows. I proceeded with care past Ballysadare and through Ballinacarrow, where a "For Sale" sign outside Jimmy G's, a pub on a wooded half acre with a three-bedroom house, caught my eye. I parked on the main street, still deserted at ten o'clock except for a little terrier who befriended me, and called Padraig, the listing agent, on my cell phone. He'd tried to sell Jimmy G's at auction a month ago, but there weren't any takers. Ballinacarrow boasted two new subdivisions, the pompously named Owenmore Paddock and Temple Manor, so I assumed the land alone would be valuable, and Padraig agreed, although the pub's license also carried an intrinsic worth and would fetch about $260,000 on the open market.

Padraig couldn't imagine Jimmy G's operating as a pub again, and blamed the drink-driving laws. He hoped to sell the land and the license separately. A rural pub's license used to cost nothing because it was site-specific and couldn't be transferred to another location, but you can move it anywhere now, and that accounts for the inflated price. The figure Padraig quoted is about average and roughly equal to what you'd pay in Dublin, where a license went for about $700,000 before the new law led to parity. It isn't just would-be publicans who bid for the licenses, either. Any business that wants to sell alcohol—restaurants, hotels, supermarkets, even gas stations—is a potential buyer.

As for the campaign against drink-driving, I'd begun to wonder if it might be a knee-jerk excuse offered on behalf of pubs that were already faltering for reasons unrelated to road safety. The impact of "lifestyle changes" in rural Ireland had to be just as profound. A village such as Ballinacarrow isn't so cut off anymore. The residents of Owenmore Paddock and Temple Manor, like those in Dromod and Ballyscannel, are commuters, probably to Sligo or even Galway, and their lives are diverse and globally intertwined via the media and the Internet—Marshall McLuhan's prophecy writ large. They don't share a single core narrative as farmers do, toiling through the cycle of the seasons with their fingers crossed, so the concept of place may be incidental to their destiny. The pub as a community center and a source of oral history may be doomed in that context.

Meanwhile, I had to deal with an overly affectionate terrier. The little guy threw me doe-eyed glances and tried to jump into my car to ride shotgun, so I gave him a very gentle nudge of the toe and rolled on to Curry, where the Yeats Country Inn (as opposed to the Yeats Country Hotel & Spa in Rosses Point) dominated the scenery. In Bellaghy, Paddy Mac's was on the block, and so it continued through each town and village, with pubs keeling over before my eyes. The future belonged to the suburbs, it seemed, and not to Jimmy G's or Paddy Mac's. Fields were selling faster than licensed premises in Ireland, and you had only to check the statistics to verify it.

In 1980, there were 223,400 farms in Ireland, but only about 130,000 remain. For the most part, they're family owned and hold an average of about eighty acres, but they yield just 3 percent of the gross domestic product. The bulk of the acreage is planted to grass, with beef cattle and milk providing a little over half of the total agricultural output. Ireland is the biggest beef dealer in the EU, in fact, with nine of every ten cattle sold for export. A great many farmers are old—one in five is sixty-five or over—and unmarried, so they have no children to succeed them. Farmers who do have families often find that their offspring are as reluctant as publicans' kids to follow in their footsteps. Though farming can sometimes be lucrative, it's usually a struggle, and most farmers work a second job to pay the bills.

To be a farmer in modern Ireland, you need computer skills and high-speed broadband access, as well as a tractor and a mower. The ability to download complicated government forms and unscramble the instructions is a necessity. Without the subsidies farmers receive from both the state and the EU, they'd be in an even deeper mess. Under the Rural Environmental Protection Scheme, a program to reduce overstocking, erosion, and the runoff of nitrates that pollute the Shannon and other rivers, the average farm gets about $10,000 a year. Grants from the EU used to be pegged to production, but they're geared to the acreage planted now, so you earn the same amount regardless of what you grow or husband, and that makes it tougher on little farms.

The fierce attachment of the Irish to the land, documented with such fidelity in John B. Keane's *The Field*, may be fading fast, along with the agrarian life. There are still some Bull McCabes around, headstrong, brutal men who'll battle to hang on to their rocky patch, but they, too, are a dying breed. (Keane's play is based on the case of Moss Morris, an American bachelor farmer, whose neighbor was suspected of murdering him in a dispute about the position of a fence.) As I crossed over from Sligo to east Mayo, though, and skirted the fringe of Knock, a devotional shrine ever since the Virgin Mary materialized on the gable of a parish church in 1879, the countryside was so orderly and serene that you'd never guess the farms, each precisely demarcated by dry stone walls, were in trouble.

From Claremorris I drove southwest through Ballinrobe until I reached Cong, population 150. The village loomed so large in the romantic view of Ireland that I hadn't expected it to be so small. It felt like a place beyond which lay nothing—an ethereal, watery place. *Cung* in Gaelic means a narrow strip of land, and Cong does seem to float on a thin isthmus between Loughs Corrib and Mask, both rich in salmon and brown trout, as is the Cong River. The Augustinian monks at Cong Abbey, founded in 1120 by Turlough Mor O'Connor, an Irish high king and the ruler of Connacht, constructed a fishing hut over the river, with a trap door for hoisting up their catch. They ran a cord to the abbey's kitchen, and when they yanked it, a bell rang to alert the cooks to light a fire.

Tourist season was almost over in Cong, as it had been in Yeats Country. I covered the village on foot in a matter of minutes. Pat Cohan's pub was closed at three in the afternoon, alas, but the Quiet Man Cottage Museum, a whitewashed, thatched replica of Sean Thornton's White O'Mornin', readily admitted me. (The actual cottage, now a ruin, is in Malm Cross, thirteen miles away.) For five euros, I was treated to "authentic reproductions" of the Duke and Maureen O'Hara's costumes, Thornton's dresser and bed, and a tandem bicycle the lovers rode. (Even as I write these words, I can't believe I traveled to Cong and paid five euros to gape at a replica of a tandem bike.) The exhibits were nicely curated, but I drew the line at John Wayne's shoes. As base as it sounds, I'd rather have spent the fiver on a pint at Pat Cohan's.

Perhaps the Quiet Man pub would meet my needs and rectify the situation, I thought, but I circled Cong twice, reading signs and peering at storefronts, without seeing a trace of it. The pub was too quiet—it was invisible, or known only to the initiates of the QM Movie Club, possibly a secret society with a special handshake and a coded language. Nobody in town had heard of it, either. Could the bar's components still be moldering in a Hollywood warehouse or, worse, an attic in Cong? Ryan's pub *was* open, but it had no customers because the barman had cranked up Led Zep's "Stairway to Heaven" to a decibel-shattering level. Barry Fitzgerald, in his role as the leprechaun-like Michaleen, would've thrown a fit.

Forced to look elsewhere for amusement, I roamed through the Quiet Man Gift Shop, where the shelves were stacked with books, memorabilia, and 8" × 10" glossies of the principal actors—Victor McLaglen, Ward Bond, Mildred Natwick, you could collect the entire cast. Quiet Man aprons dangled from a rack, and there were piles of dusty, emblematic stuff you had to root through to even begin to identify. The proprietor was startlingly uninterested in me, too, given that she had no one else to wait on. A short, snippy woman with wiry black hair, she confessed to being in a bad mood, rankled by the tourists, primarily Americans, who had failed to buy her souvenirs and geegaws on the scale she'd anticipated and probably even dreamed of.

"What kind of tourists are those?" she carped. You have to imagine the Irish version of a Bronx accent, that grating sound of chalk on a blackboard. I mentioned the painfully weak dollar and alluded to its crippling effect on my own finances, casting about for a bit of sympathy she'd never extend in a bazillion years. "Iraq!" she all but shouted. "Don't go where you don't belong! Saddam kept those people in line." She cheered up, marginally, when I plucked *Guide to Quiet Man* from her treasure trove, a booklet whose author had been on Ford's set in his youth. It included info about Cong's flora and fauna, and anecdotes about the stars—Wayne in a drunken pub brawl, Bond hooking a salmon, McLaglen tearing into a juicy steak at the Imperial Hotel in Tuam, that sort of thing.

Speaking of food, the proprietor hurried me toward the door, because she was going home for lunch. She had to pick up some groceries first, but only what she could pay for in cash. She disliked credit cards and had never applied for one. "If you can't afford it, do without it," she cautioned me, then pointed to a vacant lot across the street, where an apartment complex would soon be built, Cong's first little tract. She did not approve of it, nor did she think much of some of the American women she'd met, who gorged on junk food and were often three stone, or forty-two pounds, overweight. "Eat healthy!" That was her parting advice.

She locked the door behind her, and there I stood, alone and friendless in Cong, when I could have been reading a book by the Aga and preparing for a night at Jordans. To while away the eternity that time had become, I walked through the abbey and along the river in a light drizzle until the gates of Pat Cohan's finally swung open. The pub's focus, suffice it to say, was on *The Quiet*

Man, a film I'd started to loathe, however unfairly. There were no farmers or anglers inside, just two Japanese guys with crewcuts and a limited command of English, and an Irish-American couple from Albany, who were very sweet and a fount of QM trivia. Cohan's might have gotten more spritely later on, but I'd headed for Dublin by then, kicking myself once per mile.

As for the mystery of the Quiet Man pub, Paddy Rock of the QM Movie Club, who leads tours of the film's locations, solved it for me. The story about the club importing Ford's prop bar from Hollywood was inaccurate, he told me on the phone, yet Paddy and his mates did intend to turn Pat Cohan's into an authentic reproduction of its cinematic equivalent. (My confusion over this authenticity issue was extreme by now.) They'd gone about it assiduously, too, analyzing the movie frame by frame. Gus Marshall, another club member and a pub fitter by trade, estimated that he'd studied thirty thousand blown-up stills to gauge the bar's correct dimensions. The bar, put together in Dublin, would be transported to Cong soon and installed by Marshall and his crew.

Paddy Rock sounded keyed up about the venture. He'd even devised a gimmick to launch it, although he wouldn't reveal it in advance. Instead he urged me to watch the QMMC Web site for further details. ("Pat Cohan's Bar will soon pull its first pint ever," went the most recent dispatch. In fact, the bar opened in September 2008.) To make Cong and its environs the ultimate experience for fans, Paddy needed only one more piece to complete the jigsaw puzzle, and that was the original White O'Mornin' at Malm Cross. The owner, a Californian from Orange County, had let the cottage crumble rather than release it to Paddy and his chums, who were eager to establish a trust to restore it. "Maybe you can get somewhere with him," Paddy suggested. He gave me the number, but I never called. The Californian might be holding out for a better offer from a developer with deep pockets, I figured, someone ready to build Malm Cross Meadows or White O'Mornin' Villas.

Chapter 10

A WISE MAN, INDEED

THE FOLLY OF Cong marked the low point of my journey. Some fantasies are so pernicious you can't talk yourself
out of them, even when you're aware of their probable distance
from reality. I knew better than to expect anything special from a
venture designed to rope in tourists, yet some twisted part of me
still held out a minuscule hope that the Quiet Man pub would
rise above its origins and deliver a memorable experience. Fairytale Ireland—romantic, changeless—packs a powerful punch, and
it weaves a witchy spell that keeps those plastic pubs around the
world in business. People long for the mythical kingdom of harps
and Guinness, bards and crumbling castles, where conflict doesn't
exist and Tim Finnegan wakes from the dead, buoyed back to life
by a baptismal splash of whiskey.

Fairytale Ireland, with its accent on authentic replication, is an
empire built on kitsch, but there's a good deal of hand-wringing
in its real-life counterpart at present over what it actually means
to be Irish. Identity is a slippery concept, particularly in a global
context, and the Irish feel protective toward their own, although
they're not adept at defining it precisely. Yet it's so valued and

talismanic that Síle de Valera, a former Minister of the Arts, fretted about Ireland's participation in the EU and saw it as a potential threat to the "core of our historic identity," a catchall phrase broad enough to include Tara, the Book of Kells, and the traditional pub. In fact, the Irish are far more comfortable identifying with America than with Europe. "We're closer spiritually to Boston than Berlin," Mary Harney, a prominent politician, once said.

America has always been the land of opportunity for the Irish, of course, where an immigrant can take advantage of breaks that didn't exist at home until quite recently. The component of longing in Fairytale Ireland may well have its roots in the displacement so many of the Irish endured when they left home and crossed the Atlantic to better themselves. America stands for the future, while England brings to mind the colonial past. Perhaps that accounts for the transformation of Ranelagh into a weirdly American hybrid, with Russells as our virtual Santa Monica and McSorley & Sons as our virtual Upper East Side. TriBeCa is the busiest eatery on Ranelagh Road, and Gourmet Burger is the most popular new café, but does that imply that Ireland, through its sudden boom, is becoming virtual, too, and losing its distinctive Irishness?

And what constitutes Irishness, anyway? When the *Irish Times* asked its readers to list six aspects of it some years ago, the question prompted a spate of self-deprecatory humor salted with liberal lashings of the truth. Among the traits mentioned were an innate ability to talk about the weather; a natural capacity for arriving late; being a Roman Catholic and harboring a slight suspicion that sex is still a sin; a love of the horse races; the spontaneous singing of ballads; a string of relatives in the U.S.; a tendency to exaggerate; and a strong desire to avoid marriage before forty (men only). Yet the single factor referred to most often was the pub, as in knowing what time it closes; an unnatural capacity for drink, especially the late one; an inside knowledge of the local public house; and the inability to leave public houses before closing time.

My quest, conceived in very simple terms, had evolved into something far more complicated and not so easy to resolve. I felt guilty about my rash decision to abandon Sligo, too, and thought I'd make amends by exploring the fertile agricultural areas of County Kildare, where the soil is kinder than rocky Connacht's and farming is still a bread-and-butter activity. After careful consideration, I drew up a plan and promised to stick to it, regardless of the potential distractions. The town of Athy was on the menu for certain, because it's known for the sheer quantity of its pubs. Athy ("a thigh," as Joyce has it) is also the malting capital of Ireland, where barley is processed and dispatched to Guinness and other brewers. Before that, though, I'd visit Ballitore, a village settled by some Quakers from Yorkshire in the late sixteenth century, whose exploits I'd read about in the work of Mary Leadbeater, one of the first Irish women writers to appear in print.

I set out on an October morning with a hint of winter in the air, glad to be on the road again and putting the Cong episode behind me. Like the batter who strikes out in the bottom of the ninth with the bases loaded, I wanted to improve my game. In spite of the chill, the fields of Kildare were a delight to see, so crisp in the clear light and stocked with horses, sheep, and cattle. Cows have been a fixture on Irish farms since the Pagan Iron Age, at least, when they were esteemed as gifts and accepted as currency.

You could pay a debt with a cow, or tender one in tribute. On St. Patrick's list of "heinous crimes," those against cows occupied the top three spots—killing trained oxen, burning byres and cattle enclosures, and rustling.

Geographers divide Kildare into three regions. To the north lies the portion of racing fame, an imposing swath of stud farms, hunt clubs, grand Georgian estates, and green pastures. Here you find both the Curragh and the National Stud, whose founder, Colonel William Hall Walker, believed horses were subject to the same astrological forces as human beings. Walker's stallion boxes, still in use, have lantern roofs that open to allow the moon and stars to exert their influence. To the west of Kildare are the huge peat bogs that once stretched all the way to the Shannon, and to the south, where Ballitore is located, tillage farms are common.

Mary Leadbeater described the village as "encompassed by gently rising hills, except where the river Griese takes its meandering course . . . to its union with the Barrow near Jerusalem, a little hamlet in the country of Kildare. Ballitore derives its name," she went on, "from its former marsh condition ['bally' in Irish signifies a town or village, and 'togher' a bog] from which it was reclaimed by drainage and careful cultivation." Those responsible for the groves, orchards, and thick hedgerows were Mary's forebears, the Yorkshire Quakers, who did the planting in a vale "very barren of trees."

Abraham Shackleton, Mary's grandfather, created an extraordinary school in Ballitore in 1726. It housed between fifty and sixty boarders, and also took in day students. The boarders came from as far away as the West Indies. Mary recorded how Jesse Balrieves, a Jamaican, woke to his first snowy morning and shouted to his dorm mates, "O boys! See all the sugar!" Two other lads from the islands were so "small and lively" that her mother literally pinned them to her apron to prevent them from harm. Mary, the only girl at the school, could read at the age of four and later captured the rowdy atmosphere of recess in a poem:

> And now the school approaching near,
> A humming noise salutes the ear,
> The door unbarred with mirth and glee,
> They rush and hail sweet liberty,
> With rosy cheeks and laughing eyes,
> Each to his dear amusement hies.

Napper Tandy, the revolutionary, and Edmund Burke, the political philosopher, were among Shackleton's illustrious pupils. Burke became a close friend of Mary's father, Richard, and traveled from London to Ballitore on occasion with his wife, who once caused a sensation by stepping from her coach without a bonnet. Mary, observing from a nursery window as a little girl, expressed her shock at the sight of a woman with "no covering on her head but her beautiful unadorned auburn tresses." Mrs. Burke, who moved in sophisticated circles, explained that she dressed "conformably to her husband's taste," although she donned a hat of sorts for appearance's sake the next day.

Mary's own husband, William Leadbeater, landed at the school as a Huguenot orphan, and joined the Quakers "perhaps unconsciously attracted by an attachment he formed . . . to the youthful subject of this memoir," as a biographer of Mary's put it. She bore William four children, actively opposed slavery, labored on behalf of the poor, and rose an hour or so before dawn to steal some time to write. A volume of her poetry came out in 1808, but it's *The Annals of Ballitore*, compiled just before her death from dropsy, that most impressed me with its mix of whimsy and intelligent commentary. Fairies had no luck entrancing the villagers, Mary informs us, because they were too learned and pious. She also took note of the first Jew to arrive in Ballitore—Emmanuel Jacob, an itinerant con man, who showed off a fake mandrake root in a glass case to fleece a few shillings from the gullible.

The *Annals* paints such a charming, pastoral portrait of a society in harmony that I hoped I might still encounter traces of it, but Mary Leadbeater wouldn't know Ballitore now. Though the village is only a mile or so from a highway, it feels remote, as if it's been bypassed and forgotten. It isn't ugly or rundown, just dormant somehow. Apart from the three pubs I meant to try, the only business on the town square is a franchised convenience store. A ruined stone building, weeds sprouting through its roof, stands as an emblem of Ballitore's past, while the Abbyfield tract ("Fabulous new semi-detached houses, easy commuting distance to Carlow, Newbridge, Kildare, Dublin . . .") represents its future. Shackleton's school, closed in 1836, has long since gone to dust.

To see the countryside Mary loved, you must take a side road out of the village. I did it on foot, a welcome bit of stretching after the drive. The afternoon, though cool, offered plenty of sunshine. I had walked no more than fifty yards before a sweet farm landscape wrapped itself around me, its fences posted with warnings to city folks that I was happy to heed—"Beware of the Bull," for instance. By late afternoon, I'd covered about five miles and returned to Ballitore in a virtuous state of mind, ready for a well-deserved "victory" pint, but the only pub open was Kelly's or Kirwan's. It seemed to go by both names, judging by the mismatched signs.

As thirsty as I was, I couldn't handle Kelly/Kirwan. A pint would taste of defeat, not victory. Formula One races played on the TV, flashy cars were going down in flames, and a lone drinker hunched over the bar in a slump-shouldered posture of misery. Some youths were hanging out there, as well, and probably racking their brains for a solution to the boredom that might afflict any kid growing up in Ballitore, population 750. The other pubs, O.Connor and E. Butterfield, looked more favorable, so I spent some time at the Quaker Museum instead and talked about California with Mary Malone, the librarian, who'd toured it that summer and confessed to a fantasy about sitting behind the wheel of a big rig. At Harris Ranch in the Central Valley, where truckers stop to eat steaks the size of small children, she had almost climbed into a vacant cab but lost her nerve at the last minute.

Having admired Mary Leadbeater's writing desk and her statue in the garden, I gravitated toward O.Connor and E. Butterfield, but they were still locked up tight at five o'clock. They might open around six, a clerk at the convenience store advised me, although she wasn't certain. I wouldn't be going back to Dublin that night, obviously, so I drove to nearby Moone and booked a room at the High Cross Inn, where I demonstrated some laudable restraint. The inn's bar was named for Moscow Flyer, a champion steeplechase horse I once enjoyed an interspecies chat with—but that's another story, as they say—and I could have begged off Ballitore, asked the non-traditional Polish barmaid for a Guinness, and pulled up a chair by the coal fire, but my intuition and the specter of Cong—of failure—wouldn't let me.

At six o'clock, I sat in the car with the heater on full blast and stared at Ballitore's deserted streets, like a cop on a fruitless stake-out. Had my intuition been wrong? Possibly the pubs weren't in business anymore, new fatalities in the general demise. E. Butter-field resembled a defunct stable with its green half-door, above which a faded harp was faintly visible. The pub itself seemed to be fading into eternity. O.Connor was more substantial, a row house with neighbors on either side to keep it from falling over. Still, I was about to head back to the High Cross Inn when, precisely at 6:47 P.M., the lights switched on at O.Connor and someone pushed open the front door.

I did not quite sprint toward the door, but you could call it a speed-walk. "You're lucky," the publican said wryly, sensing my eagerness. "I don't usually open until seven." This was Pat O'Connor, the licensee since 1955, whose grandfather had estab-lished the pub, formerly a Quaker-owned hardware store, around 1870. The space was utilitarian, with an interior of scrap ma-hogany Pat's carpenter father, Joseph, had constructed. Farmers don't ordinarily subscribe to *House Beautiful* or dwell on ques-tions of aesthetics or design, so the pub showed a disregard for any aspect of the fanciful. The look was spare and unprepossess-ing, with a long front bar and a lounge at the back, once the fam-ily kitchen, that could not be said to encourage lounging.

Pat O'Connor had a knack, perhaps genetic, for being instantly likable. You couldn't be around Pat for a nanosecond without feel-ing warmer toward the human race. When he brought my pint, a symbol as potent to me by now as the glass of water a desert rat seizes upon, he asked how old I thought he was. This is a trick question, of course, since nobody who looks their age (or older) ever puts it to you, so you have to factor in some flattery and adjust the estimate accordingly. I put Pat at a well-preserved seventy-five. He was short and reasonably trim, and his thinning hair, combed straight back, was still jet-black with no telltale hint of a cheap dye job. He had a quick wit, savored a joke or an anecdote, and laughed readily at the world and his own foibles. He carried himself in an untroubled way, too, as if the aches and pains of aging had granted him a free pass so far.

I did the math, factored and adjusted. "Early seventies?"

"I'll be eighty soon." He sounded proud, really pleased with himself. To be eighty and in good health was an unexpected gift.

Though Pat was a native of Ballitore, he'd tried to escape from it several times. He knew Ranelagh, and had boarded with an aunt there as a young man, while he worked as an apprentice barman in Booterstown on the marshes by the Irish Sea. He might have stayed, but he was drawn back home when electricity reached the village in the 1940s. (The first item to be electrified in most rural houses was a Sacred Heart lamp.) He couldn't remember the exact year, so he slipped through a door behind the bar and into his living quarters. "When did we get the electricity, Sally?" he asked his wife.

"Nineteen forty-seven," I heard her say.

Pat had been twenty then and full of beans, and he took over an old Quaker barn in a field behind the pub that had been used as a cinema. That's what he called it—the Cinema. "Not very original," he admitted. He ran movies twice a week, every Wednesday and Sunday, often to a packed house. Sunday was a guaranteed sellout, because it gave the men who'd been drinking all day, starting right after Mass, an opportunity to regain some face. The pub was required by law to close at seven, so the men dutifully escorted their wives to the eight o'clock feature. The Cinema flourished into the 1970s, but it finally lost out to television. Meanwhile, Pat helped at the pub, too, and learned from his dad, who taught him the tricks of the trade, such as how to cope with an obstreperous customer who's three sheets to the wind.

"You can see it coming," he contended, and again I imagined a publican as the captain of a ship, capable of steering his way to safety through a storm. "You let him shout at you a few times, but you pretend not to hear him, and he gets the message sooner or later. You never confront him, though. That's the worst thing to do! If you tell a man he's overdone it, he'll deny it. He'll be indignant and insist, 'I've not had too much!' You need the temperament for it." He was referring to an inner calm, the peacemaker's ability to restore order. "When somebody's growlin' at you, you don't go too near him."

Currently, Pat's regulars include the elderly, the unemployed, and day laborers rather than farmers. The unemployed astound him, because they always have the price of a drink. As for the kids who hang out at Kelly/Kirwan, they never bother with his pub. "We only offer company," he told me. "With the elderly"— a category from which he cleverly excluded himself—"a lot of these people are dying," he went on, with his eyes twinkling. "You expect so-and-so to stroll in, and instead somebody says, 'He's dead, and *he's* dead, and *he's* dead.'" Pat reeled off the litany in a spirit of high hilarity. He could probably squeeze an ounce of mirth from a broken leg.

Maybe Pat's sense of humor kept him going. He didn't need the money, really. He and Sally had even tried to retire not long ago, but they failed miserably. They bought a house in Dublin and managed to keep busy during the day, doing the shopping and running errands, but the nights were intolerable, so quiet and lonely with the two of them parked before the telly and no buzz anywhere. They had never had to hunt down a conversation before— the conversation came to them at the pub. They lasted only a month in the city, then rented out their place. "We were just proddin' at it, like," Pat said, applying some spin to the adventure. "Isn't that right?" he asked Sally, who'd joined us at the bar. She's an ideal match for her husband, smart and reflective, honest and ingratiating, another native of Ballitore.

Sally remembered the exhilirating times they'd had together in the old days, when they would gather up some bottles after the pub closed and attend a house dance at the home of Jimmy Gibbons, a wizard fiddler. (The church disapproved of such dances because they could lead to sins of the flesh.) They cleared out the furniture and drank and danced until dawn, and the last dance was always a waltz. Ballitore was still a true village then, with a tailor, a cobbler, and a "high-class" draper; two hardware stores and three groceries; a bicycle shop that also sold radios; butchers and greengrocers; two ice cream parlors; and so on. People walked to O.Connor or rode a bike, Sally said, and they were all neighbors, so they had to behave agreeably. A publican could exercise control by a type of moral suasion. Now plans were on the books to build an apartment complex for forty low-income families, along with 130 houses in a tract similar to Abbyfield.

The pub wasn't so neighborly anymore, and Pat missed the

characters who used to drop in, eccentrics who were never bland or boring and told terrific whoppers. "Oh, they could make it up!" he exclaimed. "The half of it was lies!" One regular had a repertoire of ghost stories, and you were sure to be his target if he knew you'd be heading home along the path by the Quaker cemetery. And speaking of characters, what about that scurrilous gang of writers at McDaids, where Pat drank at times during the war years? "The gibberish they talked! Patrick Kavanagh, and that other clown, what was his name?"

I took a stab. "Brendan Behan?"

"That's it! Brendan Behan!"

I leaned toward Pat, keen to hear literary history rewritten.

"Brendan Behan, he was a terrible blatherer," he said, with relish. "Always shoutin' and roarin' and carryin' on. They'd be talkin' a load of rubbish, and now they're God Almighty! Only Paddy O'Brien could put up with that lot. He was the perfect barman!"

O'Brien had led the flight of the faithful, I recalled. "What made him perfect?"

"He believed in those fellas for some reason. Paddy couldn't see the bad in people. He accepted them as they were, always lettin' them drink without payin'. 'I'll have to put this on the tick,' they'd say. Behan, he swapped Paddy a couple of copy books for some credit once, and he rushed in lookin' for them weeks later. *Borstal Boy* was in those books, and he had an English publisher waitin' for them at a hotel, so they dug under the bar and through all the cabinets and cubbyholes until Paddy found them. Any other barman would have tossed them away."

I wished Paddy O'Brien were still around, so I could consult him. For drinkers of a certain age, he has the status of a saint, much as Matt Talbot does for the abstainers. The challenges he dodged on a daily basis would have destroyed the average barman. As an example, Pat related the tale of a mysterious stink that emanated from the gents' at McDaids. O'Brien inspected the plumbing, ordered the urinal scrubbed and disinfected, and replaced the water in the toilet, but the stink persisted. Only after tearing apart the room did he discover its source, a T-shirt stuffed behind a cistern. One of the writers ("a dirty, *filthy* fella") had stowed it there. He'd worn it all winter without washing it, then discarded it, caked and sweat-stained, in the first warm blush of spring.

At eight thirty, I was still O.Connor's only customer. E. Butterfield hadn't even opened yet and possibly wouldn't bother, according to Pat, who had a quiz slated for later on and thought it might bring in a few people. He blamed the usual culprits—"lifestyle changes" and the drink-driving laws—but the decline of rural pubs really spelled the death of the traditional Irish village, with its distinctive shop fronts (not the logos of franchises) and an economy based on farming. Suburbs and commuters were the order of the day—a sobering sight, as it were, especially for someone like me, who grew up in a 1950s Levitt house and had watched the farms of Long Island disappear as the tracts ate up Nassau and Suffolk counties. One had to wonder, too, if the houses in Abbyfield would hold their inflated value, or would merely collapse when the Tiger's roar was not so deafening.

"Strangers always say, 'Ballitore's a lovely place, I'd love to live here,'" Pat remarked as I was leaving. "If you do live here, you look up and wonder, 'What the devil are they talkin' about?'" It could be the old familiar longing for Fairytale Ireland, I thought, a condition that induces a sort of blindness. A visitor sees only

Mary Leadbeater's gently rising hills and the River Griese still meandering, although just barely, and blocks out the new developments that are making the real Ireland ever more generic, suburban, and American.

Crows. I woke to a racket of them, as black as cinders, attacking the stubble around the High Cross Inn. On my bedside table lay a copy of the *Kildare Post*, a giveaway paper I'd studied over dinner and beyond. I knew now that Athy had its first support group for gays, lesbians, and bisexuals, and that a Newbridge man who ingested magic mushrooms had been arrested for stretching out on a dark road to facilitate his trip. "It took a while to get his attention," an officer dryly noted. The tripper had twenty-three prior arrests, and since his parents had moved to the country from Dublin to put some distance between their son and "the occasion of sin," the judge was fairly lenient.

I also found a tipster's column in the *Post*. Its author, Father Sean Breen, the Racing Priest, advised his readers to back L'Antartique in the Paddy Power Gold Cup at Cheltenham "as soon as possible." I copied the tip into a notebook below a late-night entry that read, "Curiosity is its own kind of punishment," after which I'd added, "The next pub down the road may not deliver the revelation you seek." In my defense, there was a reason for the mopiness—I was tired. The bar of the inn, once so ingratiating with its coal fire and Polish barmaid, was still hopping at closing time, and sleep became a state to be yearned for but never achieved. Here, too, I must pillage my notebook for an observation of Sally O'Connor's. "The Irish have to be told to go home," she said. "Whatever is wrong with them, I'm sure I don't know."

After breakfast, I left for Athy, a place *The Rough Guide to Ireland* tends to scorn. "Prosperity has turned a handsome Georgian town with a fine main square into something much more ramshackle," the guide says, but I liked Athy at first glance. Granted, it has its share of suburban sprawl, and traffic jams as knotty as midtown Manhattan on a Friday afternoon, but it retains a distinct flavor of the farm, more so than Ballitore. As if to certify that fact, there were clumps of turf and clods of mud on the sidewalks. One farmer's car stalled on a main street had bunches of grass stuck in its bumper, clearly the result of a drive through a field to check on the livestock. The River Barrow wound through town and flowed past White's Castle, a pretty stream full of such coarse fish (non-salmon family) as roach, bream, and pike.

The Barrow meets the Grand Canal at one end of town, near a plant where barley is malted. I caught the roasted scent immediately, stronger even than at St. James's Gate. The plant had big stainless-steel tanks and throbbed with the hum of machinery. For barley growers, the times were bullish. Ireland's yield per acre has been the highest in the world for the past two years, due in part to the ideal climate. The harvest takes place in late July or early August, when the moisture content ranges from 17 to 20 percent. The Brewing Room Book at Greencore Malt admirably sums up the cereal's healing properties. The thiamine in barley may prevent beriberi, for example, while its niacin helps to thwart pellegra— good news, indeed, for nineteenth-century sailors.

In terms of pubs, Athy lives up to its reputation for quantity. On a hundred-yard stretch of William Street, I counted eight, and only one was for sale. (I noticed others later, but the damage was still minor compared to smaller villages.) You can attribute the glut to

Athy's history as a market town, once anchored in Heritage Square. If a farmer scored a substantial payday, he celebrated in the grand manner. "When they visit market towns to sell a cow or a horse, they never return home till they have drunk the price in Spanish wine . . . or Irish usquebagh, and this they have outslept two or three days drunkenness," commented Fynes Moryson, an Elizabethan writer, who despised all things Irish except the whiskey.

In Moryson's day, most farmers belonged to the ranks of the poor, and their lot had not improved by the pre-Famine era, when they were universally dependent on potatoes. The humble tuber, easy to grow in any soil and not labor-intensive, had routed most other crops, as we all know, but I'd been ignorant of the scale of the conquest. As early as 1780, Arthur Young, touring Kildare, found that a barrel of potatoes would last a family of six for only a week, averaging out to about seven pounds per person. Almost forty years later, a survey revealed a much higher rate of consumption. A typical farmer's breakfast in Rathkeale consisted of five pounds of potatoes, milk, and sometimes a little herring, and he ate the same meal again for dinner in the afternoon.

One anomaly of the Athy pub scene, as Frank Taaffe mentions in *Eye on Athy's Past*, is the number of pubs strategically located on the edge of town, so that "bona fide travelers" could drink at them after hours. To be bona fide, you had to travel in good faith for at least three miles from wherever you had stayed the night before, as measured by a road or a footpath. A publican was obliged to serve you regardless of the time—and apparently did so gladly. (J. M. Synge uses the bona fide gambit in *The Playboy of the Western World*, where the boozers all follow a long, complicated, three-plus-mile route to the shebeen.) The law, scrapped in 1953, forbade anyone from traveling strictly for refreshment, an unenforceable clause flouted with impunity after cars entered the picture. Brian O'Nolan, in the guise of Myles na gCopaleen, liked to say he'd driven himself to drink.

On Woodstock Street, I spotted Willie Doyle's and looked in just as the clock struck noon, not yet ready for a pint and even put off by the idea after my sleepless night, but I represented a minority of one. Doyle's has three little rooms, and each was as densely occupied as a hive, with the regulars already gearing up for a long afternoon of televised racing and the betting that goes with it. An old saw has it that the best location for a pub is next to a church; the second-best might be near a bookie joint, and here Doyle's was truly blessed, with two shops across the street. All day the regulars would shuttle back and forth, inadvertently testing their sobriety as they dodged a steady barrage of cars and trucks to get down a wager.

In every town like Athy, there's a pub (or six) such as Doyle's, where the anguished curses of losers and the raucous bray of winners form the very fabric of a Saturday afternoon. The bookies thrive on the action, of course. They're not devious types who operate from a dingy dive anymore. Instead, they're often corporate titans, and their shops can be ritzy. Boylesports, where I placed a bet in advance on Swiss Cottage in the three o'clock race at Naas, another of Father Breen's tips, was so bright and merry that the staff might have been handing out free twenty-euro bills. The fog of broken dreams that makes breathing difficult had yet to collect. The doomed gambler of yesteryear—unshaven, in a stained trenchcoat, trying to cash a rubber check—was nowhere to be seen.

Boylesports was even "child-friendly," and I almost cuffed a toddler by accident, when he grabbed my calf while I checked the racing paper. In their nifty uniforms, the young women cashiers could be mistaken for the cabin crew on a plane, devoted to your safe arrival wherever on the mental map that might be. Should your bladder seize up during a race, there's a TV over the urinals. If you lose a massive bet and develop a sudden case of Tourette's syndrome, Boylesports probably has a medic on call to treat you. The shop's only drawback is the absence of alcohol—hence, the beauty of Willie Doyle's.

As comfortable as I might have been at Doyle's, patiently explaining to the lads why I shouldn't have listened to the Racing Priest after Swiss Cottage finished a well-beaten fifth, I fought off temptation and looked for a less hectic, more traditional pub instead. (To Father Breen's credit, L'Antartique did win at Cheltenham.) I passed up the Nag's Head and Clancy's, Kane's and Brian Smith's, all decent but undistinguished, and circled Ann's Place, where a tortoise crawled across the façade of the pub with a pint balanced on its shell. "Have a Guinness when you're tired!" ran the slogan beneath it, advice I almost took until I noticed O'Brien on Heritage Square, a strikingly handsome spot that also billed itself as a grocery.

The shopfront was a work of art, with paint so fresh and unmarked it could have been touched up the day before. Twin ionic columns, bright red, supported a broad green bannerlike beam on which the name O'Brien was written in Gaelic script. Big windows on either side of the door were trimmed in the same red, and each had three panes. At the top of each pane was a single word, and when combined they read *Sweet Athy forever*. (Sweet Athy figures in the lyrics to the folk songs "Johnny, I Hardly Knew Ye" and

"We're On the Road to Sweet Athy.") Though the windows were as clean as could be, you couldn't see through them because of the cartons of Tayto chips and other dry goods stacked up behind them, almost to the ceiling.

Many pubs rely on their history as a grocery as a come on, but few still actually trade. E.J. Morrissey's in Abbeyleix, a Midlands town in County Laois, has walls covered with old, or old-appearing, tin ads for beer, tobacco, and such, and shelves laden with antique cereal boxes and canned food, but they're all just for show, as is the fellow in a white, knee-length shop assistant's coat, who circled around when I was there, as if waiting to fill an order. Nothing at O'Brien's is staged, however. Once you go through the door and step past the cartons, you're at a front counter stocked with essentials—tea, butter, eggs, whiskey, all the items a family might have bought a century ago, with the exception of the top-ups for cell phones, the new bestseller.

The pub was at the back of the shop, through a doorway. Frank O'Brien sat there on a stool behind the bar, all alone, sipping a cup of tea and eating Pringles. He belonged to Pat O'Connor's peer group, in terms of his age. (The key to longevity, I'd decided, is to be a publican, as long as you're careful not to dip into the merchandise.) Taller and slimmer, he had a vaguely academic air, that attitude of mild abstraction suggestive of an intellectual dreaminess. As men of his generation do, he wore a tie, a V-neck sweater, and a sportcoat, and probably would have felt naked without them. To keep himself company, he'd been watching *Superbrainiac* on the tube, although not closely enough to register how loud the volume was, but my presence alerted him to the din, and he hit the clicker to reduce it.

I praised the design of the shopfront and remarked on the pub's antiquity. The O'Briens have owned it since 1875, but it may be older, and Frank nodded pleasantly, too polite to say he'd heard it all before. I commented next on the glory of the day, once again bathed in radiant sunshine, and how pretty the Barrow looked to an angler. It rises in the Slieve Bloom Mountains of Laois and runs for about 120 miles to the sea, with a towpath along it where horses once pulled barges, some loaded with malted barley. Though coarse fish are its specialty, it also holds some trout, but Frank didn't think I'd hook many in Athy because of the poor water quality. "The Lordly Barrow," he said.

"The Lordly Barrow?" I repeated, a little baffled.

"Was that Spenser, or the other fella? The one with the pilgrims?"

I began to catch his drift. "Chaucer?"

"That's right, Chaucer. 'The Lordly Barrow'—I don't know which one wrote it. No memory, gone for poetry and that now."

This could be true, but Frank doesn't miss a beat otherwise. He collects books, in fact, and had attended a launch earlier that month for an illustrated one about the bridges on the Barrow. He showed me a copy, suitably inscribed by the author. He has a small library in the pub, and refers to it to settle disputes among his customers, mostly over sports trivia. (Hurling is Athy's obsession, and the fans debate its fine points heatedly.) Two young "fellas" had stopped at O'Brien's some weeks ago, Frank recalled, while they were hiking the towpath by the river—it's known as the Barrow Way—and they wondered why any publican would have so many books on hand.

"They're for lads like you that asks me questions," he told them, a direct enough answer.

"You must do a lot of reading," I said.

"A lot of skimming. Ah sure, you wouldn't have time to read, would you?"

Two girls interrupted our talk. They came in and stood by the front counter, and Frank got up and sold them some candy. He made a dozen sales over the next hour, courteous and unflappable, and also curious who the shopper might be, since he couldn't see the counter clearly from his stool. It was a sort of game he played, I thought, and through a tally of the purchases, he could tell you more about Athy than the mayor. Of a man who bought two mini-bottles of Powers whiskey, he said, "You never know, bad is good," a gnomic utterance I couldn't parse. A Nigerian stepped to the counter next, but he left empty-handed. "Looking for strap," Frank muttered. "Strap" means credit. "Funny lad, only recently in town." After the Nigerian came a woman with an infant; she asked for six slices of corned beef.

O'Brien's grocery earns about four times as much as the pub, but it's amazing that it earns any money at all, since it's besieged by supermarkets and chain stores on every corner. What you get in the bargain, though, is Frank, and the locals are willing to invest in the relationship, even if it costs a few pennies more. Frank knows the names of many customers, and he never rushes to complete a transaction and is always ready for a chat. You learn things from him, too, as I did when he urged me to attend the annual Shackleton Weekend. Ernest Shackleton, the Antarctic explorer and a descendant of Abraham Shackleton, was born in Kilkea near Ballitore, and Athy honors him every year.

Another Nigerian materialized in the shop. He distributed some fliers for the Mountain of Fire and Miracles Ministry, the

Domain of Total Deliverance and Heaven-shaking Prayers, a Lagos-based church whose Athy rep was Pastor Emmanuel Aboluwade. Frank thanked the man and piled the fliers on a potato chip carton for the moment. Students from twenty different countries were enrolled at one of the girls' schools in town, he said, and a Nigerian boy had become a star rugby player for a junior division team. Frank's cousin, a Vicentian priest, had volunteered at an orphanage about a thousand miles from Lagos, and Frank still sent an occasional donation. I'd spent time in Nigeria myself, and asked about the precise location of the orphanage.

"Have to look it up," Frank replied. "Me and the cousin, we haven't been communicating since he died."

While Frank dealt with another shopper, I peeked into the lounge off the bar, once a parlor and even less seductive than O.Connor's. A door marked "Private" led to Frank's quarters, and the pub's toilets were in the garden. When he returned to his perch, I asked if the lounge got much use. Frank looked startled, taken aback. He'd hosted two meetings there just last week, both for groups of meggers. I stared at him blankly, so he elaborated. Meggers is Athy slang for horseshoe players, and the game is a favorite among farmers, who have ample access to shoes. They're very serious, he declared, and have even traveled to the States to compete in world championships. He seemed flattered the groups had chosen O'Brien's for their deliberations.

More delicately, I inquired whether or not the pub would be busy later on. I'd been the only one at the bar all afternoon. Frank felt sure that it would be, although the hot spot on Saturday night was J. Anderson Market House across the square. Instead of a lovely painted shop front, it had a dull industrial look, and was plastered with ads for rock bands and cheap beer. "Four bouncers there." Frank smiled and tapped his chest. "Here only me." He has a daughter, who assists him all the time, so I asked if she might be the proprietor some day. He appeared to think so, but that wasn't a discussion he wished to pursue. "I work on the present," he said, a wise man, indeed.

Chapter 11

CLOSING TIME

Sunday mornings in my part of Dublin are languid, even mildly comatose. People wake to their lives with a certain reluctance. For a Californian accustomed to the footfall of joggers at dawn, it's strange to go out for coffee and find the streets empty. You feel like a gunslinger in Tombstone, whose impending duel has forced the decent folks to take cover inside. The sensation of emptiness grows stronger if the weather's awful, as it was on my return from Athy. I could almost hear my neighbors groan and bundle their heads under their pillows after they'd had a peek at the leaden sky. There's a gray in Ireland that trumps all the other grays I've ever seen, and when it casts its pall, Dubliners can be forgiven for staying in bed.

The rain, bitter-cold, did not begin until the early evening, while I was doing some errands downtown. To escape it, I took refuge at James Toner, where Yeats had sipped his sherry—just one, although Toner's implies otherwise. "It is rumored that Toner's was the only pub W. B. Yeats drank in," says its brochure, gilding the lily. "He was known to sip a sherry and leave." Here was a bid nearly as bold as Guinness's appropriation of Joyce. Is there

anywhere else on earth where writers are held in such commercial esteem? True, Shakespeare earns a nod in England, and Hem-
ingway owns Key West, but as brand-name authors they're not in
the same league as the Irish contingent, who'd have demanded
free drinks for life if they'd had a crystal ball.

Frank O'Brien and the O'Connors were still on my mind,
naturally. They were the last of their breed, so heartfelt, honest,
and witty they'd touched me deeply. The survival of their pubs—
and of rural pubs in general—had just been dealt another critical
blow, however, in the form of a new directive concerning the
drink-driving laws. There was a move to lower the permissible
level of blood alcohol even further, bringing it into line with
Sweden's ultra-strict policy, essentially one of zero tolerance. (The
Swedes don't drink much per capita—Luxembourg, Hungary,
and Ireland rank first, second, and third among EU members—
and yet they have the highest rate of drink-related fatalities on
the road.) If the new law were to be rigidly enforced, some drivers could be charged after a single beer, and the effect on isolated
pubs in the country could be devastating.

Nobody condones drinking and driving, yet it happens all the
time wherever alcohol is served. When the Irish are over the
limit, one study indicates, they don't worry about their safety or
the safety of others. What deters them is the chance that they'll
be subjected to a random test. It isn't the local cops who usually
initiate the checkpoints, though. They're orchestrated from central
command to show that the government is tackling the "carnage
on the roads." (The Christmas holidays, with their ceaseless parties, are a peak season for random testing.) The operation is high-
profile and media-friendly, conducted under the bright lights,

and though the penalties are real and severe, the exercise carries an element of public relations. Still, it's been successful enough to scare off many people including the old bachelor farmers, who've been driving to their local for years without incident, and some think that's a shame.

This "get tough" attitude is yet another aspect of the transformative dust I'd watched alter almost every facet of life in the Republic. The pace of change accelerates so briskly, without a backward glance, it can leave you stunned and breathless, as if you should be sprinting to catch up. If you blink in Ranelagh, the neighborhood may look different when you open your eyes again. Where did Papillon Skincare, a purveyor of glycolic peels and microdermabrasion, come from, anyway? What *was* a glycolic peel, and why would anyone submit to it? From the compost of decayed pharmacies and defunct shoemakers, the new shops sprout like mushrooms—expensive jewelry, art galleries, designer frocks, and stiletto heels from Italy.

No business in Ranelagh stands still for very long. Two convenience stores, a supermarket, and an off-license with a huge selection of wine had been remodeled and doubled in size in the past month. The same principle applies in the field of real estate. Any house that's sold will be done up right away. The buyers knock down walls, they build conservatories and marble-topped kitchens. What's an extra hundred grand in improvements when you've already paid a million or more for a semi-detached fixer-upper? Mario's pizzeria knocked down a wall, too, and became a trattoria with exposed brick and subdued lighting. We have Thai food, dim sum, and killer burritos on Ranelagh Road. Indeed, I'd heard the phrase "gourmet ghetto" bandied about. Only pistachio oil had fallen by the wayside, superseded by Alfonso mango, Habugo ham, and dried tomato petals.

My Irish friends approve of the changes in Ranelagh, by and large. They remember the old Ireland all too well—dominated by the church, sexually repressive, financially strapped, and removed from the cultural mainstream—so they're not disturbed by the absence of chip shops and corner markets. Pubs don't appeal to them, traditional or not, and they seldom go to one except for a sports event they can't get on cable TV, as I'd observed at Mulligan's. Instead, they prefer the upstairs wine bar at TriBeCa, where the walls are lined with cases of vintage imports, and you can have a plate of Spanish charcuterie with your bottle of Rioja. A pint of stout would seem gross in that sophisticated context, unrefined and weirdly menacing, a bellybuster to slow down rather than speed up your mental processes. For my friends, the pub is old-fashioned. It speaks of yesteryear.

The desire of most Dubliners to indulge in the same luxuries to be enjoyed in the other capitals of Europe, in Madrid or Paris, is understandable. Change is inevitable, after all, especially in a country so hungry for it, but what troubled me was the speed of change in Ireland and the unaddressed nature of it—what it means, if you will. The two-lane blacktops pressed into service as highways are a problem, but should Tara be threatened to correct it, simply to please the commuters? Isn't some ancient compact among the past, present, and future being violated, a baby thrown out with the bathwater? Like Americans, the Irish are desperate to own a home, but should the country's greenbelt be carved up and turned into one big suburb—with very little thought or advance planning—to accommodate that desire? For a developer, the land spells profit. For a farmer, the land is soil and eternal.

When I talked with my friends about what by now could only be called my obsession with the traditional pub, their eyes glazed over at times. Why bother with such an outmoded institution? They viewed me as the innocent I'd once been, the guy from California who'd seen *The Quiet Man* too often, listened to too many Van Morrison CDs, and bought into a nostalgia that John Ford, perhaps, had kicked off in 1952. Yet I still believed the traditional pub held a special significance for the Irish, and that nostalgia didn't enter into the equation. Only when I went back to the National Library after my trip to Kildare, though, and began to dig through some scholarly works on culture and identity did I find some support for my belief.

First came Walter Benjamin, scarcely a name you'll hear dropped very often at Birchall's, who had wrestled with the issue of authenticity in his essay "The Work of Art in an Age of Mechanical Reproduction." He wrote, "Precisely because authenticity cannot be reproduced"—how gratified I was to read those words!—"the arrival of certain techniques of reproduction . . . has provided the means to differentiate levels of authenticity." Authenticity is actual and original, says Benjamin, and it has an aura. It isn't in the eye of the beholder, then, despite the musings of market researchers, nor could it be attributed to Nine Fine Irishmen on the Vegas strip. The essay also explained why a trophy pub such as James Toner partakes of a measure of tradition that lifts it above most other pubs, although not quite to the level of the unspoiled ideal, where the pairing of drink and talk are supreme.

Even more instructive was a passage I found in John Berger's "Towards Understanding Peasant Experience." It struck me like a bolt from the blue, as pure enlightenment. "To dismiss peasant experience as belonging only to the past," argued Berger, "as having no relevance to modern life . . . to continue to maintain, as has been maintained for centuries, that peasant experience is marginal to civilization, is to deny the value of too much history and too many lives." The traditional pub is central to the Irish peasant experience, really, and what matters about it, maybe foremost among the qualities of Oldenburg's third place, is its characteristic democracy, where the great divide that affects all societies can be momentarily erased. It isn't nostalgic to see the traditional pub as both important and still relevant, if only as a repository for and a caretaker of Ireland's "historic identity," and its gradual disappearance may signify the loss of an authentic, irreplaceable aspect of that mystical entity called "Irishness."

Obsessions die hard. After reading Benjamin and Berger, against my better judgment, I made one more trip that December, deeper into farm country and farther away from Dublin in hopes of getting beyond the commuter rim and the city's influence. I settled on County Offaly in the Midlands, whose status as an agricultural hub had been franked that September when the National Ploughing Championships—a three-day fiesta centered around plows, furrows, and such seminars as "Market Situation for Beef and Veal at EU Level"—drew 166,000 paying customers to Annaharvey Farm in Tullamore. The county is a low-lying, boggy region on the Shannon floodplain, with two thirds of its population in rural areas and no large urban complex. The farmers have an average age of about fifty, and rear mostly sheep and beef cattle, with some dairying.

The weather was miserable again when I left the city. Martin Gale, a brilliant painter in Kildare, born in England but long resident in Ireland, conveys the gloom of a leaden sky better than anyone. For Gale, it's not only gray and impenetrable but also ominous, a heavy lid that clamps down from above and inhibits the possibility of human joy. In an essay on *Coming Storm*, a recent painting of Gale's, the poet Dennis O'Driscoll talks about how the clouds seem "hell-bent on eliminating everything radiant in their path," and that describes perfectly how the horizon looked to me.

The storm broke as I passed the Curragh, not as cold as the last but far more intense, with sheets of rain so thick I could barely see. I was relieved to get off the highway at Monasterevin and onto a lightly traveled back road to Birr, a town my guidebooks had praised. Again I was surrounded by green fields, and though the rain let up as I approached Mountmellick, another place with Quaker roots, the clouds never lifted, nor did the sky brighten. Soon the Slieve Bloom Mountains came into view, carpeted with blanket bog and densely forested, and next the attractive village of Clonaslee in County Laois, where I tried to rustle up some lunch at the only supermarket.

The sandwich counter failed to whet my appetite. It could have been the tray of previously fried and deep-fried food— chicken nuggets, wedges of potato, fatty sausages—that put me off, or maybe the sign that warned customers to eat what they purchased in the next ninety minutes or suffer the unstated consequences. To the good, the market bustled with farmers in muddy rubber boots, who groused to each other about the storm and sometimes parked a tractor out front. Tractors are big in Clonaslee. Five publications on the magazine rack pictured one on the cover, while the *Irish Farmers Journal* featured a photo of some weanling bullocks posed against a blaze of winter sun.

I considered my options. In Clonaslee, they were not unlimited. Aside from the market, the village has two small groceries, a butcher, a garage with a gas pump, and five pubs. Blooms, the only restaurant, was closed, and that left Antonio's, a classic chipper. I tend to avoid chippers for the same reason I gave up toasted sandwiches, but I was starving. Antonio is a sturdy fellow built like a fireplug, and when you order some chips, he takes his time to prepare them. They're done from scratch, so it's about a seven-minute wait. The potatoes are crucial—Maris Pipers are supposed to be the top choice—as is the temperature of the oil, but you need the skill of a master to bring all the elements together, and Antonio has it. His chips, doused with salt and vinegar, were hot, crisp, and meltingly soft within.

One pub on the main street, John Feery's Cosy Bar, happened to be open in the early afternoon, a rarity out in the country these days. It's a cheerful-looking spot, where a slogan on the façade boasts, "If you want a good drink, we serve only the best," so I rose to the bait. The Cosy Bar fit its description to a tee, being tiny, intimate, and unaffected, and T. J. Wrafter, the barman, made it even cozier by virtue of his size. Though he proved to be hospitable, he loomed large behind the taps, and when I said, "I want a good drink," I worried for a split second that he might not find me as clever as I found myself, but he just nodded, replied "Aye," and poured my Guinness.

For once I was not alone at the bar. The other customer, a taciturn farmer, was as muddy as his peers at the market. If he'd been toiling in the boggy fields since dawn, he likely deserved the large bottle of Macardles Ale that he finished almost in a gulp. He wasn't inclined to chat, so I toured Feery's and read a yellowed newspaper clip about Glebe Lad, who won the Irish Grand National in 1999. The horse belonged to a Clonaslee man, and his neighbors had backed it and cleaned out the bookies in Tullamore. Meanwhile, the parched farmer polished off another Macardles just as quickly as the first. He must be on foot or on a bike, I thought, or else unafraid of the police.

The story of John Feery's, as T. J. related it, matched those I'd heard before. His mother, Ina, is the current license holder, but none of her children except T. J., who's thirty-five, care about the pub, even though it's been in the family for almost a hundred years. The trade was slow now. Ordinarily, the bar stayed closed until tea time, but there had been a funeral that morning, and the mourners needed a nearby place where they could meet for a drink afterward, so T. J. opened as a courtesy. Once Clonaslee's main street had been dotted with shops, he recalled, just like Ballitore, but most had gone out of business. Farming was on the skids, too, in spite of the interest in tractors. New suburbs were under construction in the Slieve Blooms, and the buyers worked elsewhere—in Birr, Tullamore, Kildare, and even Dublin, a two-plus-hour commute each way.

The Laois County Council anticipated more of the same, and had said as much in its Draft Town Plan, published that month. Clonaslee is "expected to experience pressure for development over the lifetime of this plan," or the next six years, the council had concluded, and while its intentions were doubtlessly honorable, such plans are often drawn up after the genie's already escaped from the bottle. The rush hours were treacherous, T. J. told me, because the local roads, no wider or better lit than those in rural Sligo, must deal with speeders, tailgaters, farm machinery, the occasional runaway chicken or cow, and, most dangerously, cyclists and pedestrians. Through November 2007, Ireland had recorded 288 traffic deaths that year, with 29 percent of the victims hit by a car rather than driving or riding in one. No wonder the people walking their dogs in Clonaslee wore bright-yellow reflector vests in broad daylight.

A second farmer arrived at the Cosy Bar. He was in his seventies, with cheeks ruddy from exposure. He'd dressed up for the visit to town in a flat cap and a tie, concerned about his appearance and dignified in manner. His voice sounded thin and creaky, like the rusty hinge of a little-used door, when he asked T. J. for a large, or double, whiskey.

"Dirty old day," he said to me, lifting the glass in a toast.

"Awful."

"That rain!"

"All the way from Dublin."

He paused for a sip and coughed, wiping his mouth with a handkerchief. "I live up in the mountains."

"You must have lived up there for a while," I said.

He smiled. "The whole time."

The whole time. His words affected me. There'd be no other time for him, and no other place. Clonaslee constituted his whole universe, the be-all and end-all of his existence, but the village he'd always known was fading away, like the clipping about Glebe Lad. The figures in Martin Gale's paintings, often portrayed in a field, look confused and unsure of themselves, as if a purpose they'd once grasped firmly had slipped through their fingers, and the old farmer shared that uncertainty. He had nothing more to say. He downed his whiskey in a swallow, adjusted his cap, and went out the door.

The drink-driving laws had hurt Feery's, of course. The local cops exercise good judgment, T. J. said, but the customers still worry about a random test. On weekends, the Cosy Bar used to attract folks from ten different villages, who swapped gossip and played music, but that was impossible now. T. J. is a realist, though, and unsentimental. You can't drink and drive, period. Clonaslee couldn't support five pubs anymore, either, he believed. Maybe his regulars would adapt and rely on taxis, but human nature probably dictated against it. People want what they want, after all, even if it's only a good drink, and they want it right away. In fact, the Wrafters had already listed the Cosy Bar with a real estate agent very quietly, without a sign out front—the pub; a seven-bed, two-bath house; and about an acre of land, price on application.

The sky was still gray and even darker when I resumed the drive through the Slieve Blooms to Birr. The mountains, limestone layered over older red sandstone, are just hills, really, with the highest peak topping out at about 1,700 feet, but the range is seductive in a low-impact way, cut through with streams, waterfalls, and hiking trails. In spite of the weather, I took a break and walked along the Silver River by Cadamstown in Offaly, hard by the John Dempsey pub (closed), the hamlet's only business, and savored the rain-freshened air. If you were to depart from Dempsey's at night, the forest with its trove of mysteries might well play upon your mind. Which trail leads toward home? What's that noise in the thicket? Where did I put my cell phone? Here was the very moment that gives birth to those ghost stories.

"I woke one morning at eight A.M.," a woman at the Tullamore Active Retirement Association told Fearga Kenny, who collected such tales for a book, "and I was in a strange place. I saw the whole of a dog with a small black head in the room. It was a fairy dog!" Fortunately, she recovered from her fright, because those who cling to it will be dead in a year, legend has it. In the villages of Offaly, there was frequently a house with a room locked in perpetuity to keep the ghosts inside. Strong men yanked on the knob, but the door wouldn't budge. Ghost trains glided down the railroad tracks, a headlight visible in the distance, only to disappear. A driver bound for Dublin once picked up four hitchhikers, but they vanished before he reached the city—ghosts of those who'd been killed at *the exact intersection* where he met them.

The elderly of Tullamore were superstitious, too. As children, their biggest fear had been to spot a single magpie. "One for sorrow, two for joy," as the nursery rhyme goes, so they'd shudder and hide their eyes until a parent told them that the magpie had a mate—they just couldn't see it. As adults, they were spooked by redheads, who stood for bad luck. (In a curious reversal, black cats meant good luck.) If a redhead crossed your path while you were traveling, it was better to turn around and go home. Red in general was a forbidding color. You tempted fate if you wore it above green, but if you found a spider on your clothes, you'd soon receive a new coat. Spiders were a symbol of Our Lord, and were never swatted or squashed.

There was no sign of life at Dempsey's after my walk, so I continued on to Birr. As previously mentioned, I had disagreed with my *Rough Guide* over its treatment of Athy, so I'd brought along my *Lonely Planet*, as well, to provide a second opinion. I've never had much faith in guidebooks, though, and such faith as I did have soon evaporated. "Birr is a little gem, with beautifully restored Georgian streets, classy accommodation options and excellent restaurants," asserted the *Lonely Planet*, while the *Rough Guide* weighed in with another laudatory assessment, "A truly delightful Georgian town, with wide, airy streets and finely detailed, fan-lit houses."

For a brief moment, I believed it would all come true. On the outskirts of Birr, I spied a grand house with exquisite grounds, the sort of estate that suggests masked balls and kegs of three-hundred-year-old port in the cellar, but the illusion did not last long. Guidebook writers practice a form of corrupted honesty and often commit what Our Lord calls a sin of omission. There may be fan-lit houses and classy accommodations in Birr, but the streets were too blocked and congested to get anywhere near them. Of the town's 3,500 residents, approximately 3,468 seemed to be out for a spin. Instead of basking in Georgian glory, I sat gridlocked in the midst of cars, motorcycles, buses, bicycles, and obscenely large trucks—fifty, sixty, even seventy feet long—loaded with a hellish variety of freight.

One truck carried huge concrete berms—highway dividers, perhaps, each balanced precariously on a flatbed—and when the driver tried to bulldoze his way into a more strategic position in front of me, a voice from the *Nine O'Clock News* rang in my ear. "In Birr this afternoon, an American was crushed to death in a freak accident," the voice said gravely, and that led to a spike in my paranoia. To calm myself, I fixed my gaze on Dooly's Hotel in

Emmet Square, where the Galway Hunt Club, celebrating during a stay in 1809, partied with such enthusiasm that they burned down Dooly's and have been known forever after as the Galway Blazers.

In the end, I panicked. Rather than risk a turn onto Birr's equally clogged main drag, I shot through a minuscule gap in the grid toward Banagher, sure to be less harried. I felt better right away, able to breathe again, on the open road once more. Banagher is more compact, I told myself, indulging in a pep talk, and will be easier to negotiate. It's a historic market town, I also told myself, and it has literary resonances. Trollope wrote *The Macdermots of Ballycloran*, his first novel, while he worked as a postal clerk, and Charlotte Brontë spent her honeymoon there by the Shannon. Moreover, the public houses have a notoriety that can be traced back to the livestock fairs of the eighteenth century. Banagher—I was going to love it.

Those livestock fairs were rowdy events. They left the streets cluttered with dung and kept the shopkeepers, who boarded up their windows, on edge. Porter was the beverage of choice, with whiskey as its partner in crime. One farmer involved in a stabbing incident reportedly drank a gallon of porter before noon, although he denied the charge—only a half gallon, he swore. As for the knife, he'd been cleaning his pipe with it, and lashed out in a reflex action when a ruffian attacked him. If a farmer closed a deal with a hand clasp and a gob of spit—too many different dialects were spoken for a common language to exist—he was entitled to drink up the proceeds and would hire a boy to stand barefoot in the manure and mind his stock while he imbibed.

For the impoverished of Banagher, life was hard, particularly for those who were old and alone. If they fell sick or developed an infirmity, they wound up at a hideous poorhouse in Birr that did its best to dispose of its clients even before they got there. A one-eyed drunk drove the van that collected the downtrodden, and it was pulled by a one-eyed horse, possibly in the same condition. The driver hit every bump and pothole on purpose, hoping to kill off the passenger. If he failed in his mission, his "nurse" often finished the job by placing a mattress on top of the poor (in every sense) victim, lying on it, and smothering him.

"Banagher is a great little spot on the banks of the River Shannon, fast becoming a boaters' favorite thanks to the buzzing new marina." That was the *Lonely Planet*'s verdict. "It's rapidly turning into a relaxed and elegant tourist center for the Irish Midlands," concurred the *Rough Guide*. Maybe on a mild July afternoon, with no Martin Gale special effects overhead, you might ignore the eerie, gigantic plant of Banagher Concrete, Ltd. at the gateway to the town, but it was a spoiler for me, and so, too, were the streets, just as congested as Birr's. At the marina, I listened for a buzz, yet all I heard was the clank of bells and the chafe of ropes as the docked boats rocked on the tide. I wished I'd never left Clonaslee, and since that was a wish I could actually fulfill, I turned around and headed back.

Obsessions die hard, and so do fantasies. To avoid the mayhem in Birr, I took a side road to Cloghan and crawled toward Tullamore, Offaly's big city, ready for a shot of Tullamore Dew whiskey, its signature product, to calm my nerves. (The "dew" stands for Daniel E. Williams, once the brand's general manager and part-owner. His initials featured in a famous advertising slogan, "Give every man his Dew.") Despite Tullamore's size, the traffic flowed smoothly compared to what I'd experienced elsewhere. There were trucks on the streets, but they didn't function as instruments of torture, so I had a quick look around downtown, where the first Christmas lights were blinking merrily, and noticed a building on Kilbride Street with a thatched roof.

This was the Mallet Tavern, the oldest pub in Tullamore. It predated and had survived the great fire of 1785, when a hot air balloon crashed and torched about a hundred houses on nearby Patrick Street and much of Kilbride Street, too. The tavern is whitewashed, with a blackish thatch of either reeds, heather, or straw—I couldn't tell. All I knew about such roofs was that thatchers are hard to locate and reputed to share a finicky, artistic temperament. They're difficult to pin down about the timing of a job, because they're in such demand, and everybody wants to be next in line. The best way to engage a thatcher's sympathy, they say, is to engineer a "chance" meeting at a job site and admire his craftsmanship, thereby promoting yourself in his eyes.

I must accept a degree of blame, potentially large, for the expectations I laid upon the Mallet. I'd put the *Quiet Man* business to rest in Cong, after all. Why did I imagine that I'd be greeted by a glowing hearth rather than the worn green felt of a pool table? Even for a fantasist, the blast of heavy metal was a cruel shock at that hour, although the sleepy patrons seemed not to care. They were a midnight crew forced to operate in full daylight, the type of guys and gals, all five of them, you might run into at a bar in Chicago after the Bears had lost to the Packers— downbeat, that is. As for a jolly publican, forget about it. The youth on duty refused to field any questions about the Mallet's noble history.

Only Blooms offers rooms in central Clonaslee, ten clean but spartan cells above the restaurant, still closed that night, but I'd reached Damien, the proprietor, by phone, and he agreed to put me up, anyway, although there would be no other guests. He could supply a bed but no breakfast, so he knocked ten bucks off the price to drop it into the Motel Six range, then gave me the keys to the front door and took off. Alone in the echoing silence, I could have been mistaken for a character in a low-budget remake of *The Shining*. Had it really come to this? Maybe curiosity truly is its own kind of punishment. Just yesterday, I'd been reading Walter Benjamin on authenticity, and now I was about to march to Antonio's for a chicken burger and another portion of chips prepared by the maestro's son, a slimmer, fitter, jauntily pierced version of his dad.

Night had fallen in the Slieve Blooms. The streets were quiet now, and a fine, elegiac mist colored the air. You could feel an element of surrender in it, that sensation of old Clonaslee fading away. A gang of bored high school boys stood outside the supermarket, each in a hooded sweatshirt. They were full of attitude and determined to ignore the drizzle, too tough by half to let a little rain disturb their macho pose. They couldn't drink legally, but they'd scored some cigarettes and smoked with a practiced cool, spitting between puffs and nudging the sidewalk with a toe. Whenever an older boy wheeled by in a car and blew his horn, they roused themselves for a salute, pumping their fists and leaning hopefully toward the driver as they might toward a cherished vision of the future.

The Mallet had left me so shaken I almost reneged on the mini-pub crawl I'd assigned myself as a last-ditch effort to make the trip worthwhile. I had to steel myself to begin, inching into Fallons for a pint, where I read the *Irish Farmers Journal* and admired the weanling bullocks. Fallons was as quiet as the night and very friendly with a wholesome, Rotarian attitude, the kind of pub that a chess club might embrace for its weekly meeting. It hosts music sessions on Thursdays, but this was a dead Tuesday, and there was no rustle in the atmosphere to suggest the craic might descend later, either, so I crossed over to the Cosy Bar, ready to surprise T. J. and be welcomed like a prodigal son. T. J. wasn't around, though, and the farmers were gone. For company, I had five strapping jocks who drank Buds and watched a soccer match, while the barman sent text messages with his cell phone.

As I departed, McDermotts Clonaslee Inn next door abruptly came to life, an event that couldn't have been predicted by its ramshackle exterior. You could be forgiven for thinking it had slipped over the brink and now rested in peace, but a small group of men were at the bar, some farmers among them, all hefty fellows built on the T. J. scale, and they nodded affably when I joined them. They were involved in the *Nine O'Clock News*, the same program I'd earlier figured would be broadcasting my obituary live from Birr, and they talked not so much to each other as to the TV. A story about three Dublin housewives who picked up a shipment of cannabis at the airport, got lost on the way home, asked the police for directions, and were arrested kept them howling.

The jibes and pokes evoked the fun-loving quality of frat house banter, where everyone riffs on the absurdity of it all. When the news ended, I assumed the talk would turn to other subjects, but the TV stayed on and remained a major player. There were asides, of course, and the men employed a verbal shorthand that I couldn't grasp at times, so I probably missed some nuances, but my amusement still dwindled along with my beer. An archaeologist could do some fruitful work at McDermotts, it occurred to me as I glanced around, perhaps starting in the gents' toilet where a Baege Super Hand Dryer from an epoch when such machines were heralded as a technological breakthrough was nailed to a wall. A set of instructions was even posted for the uninitiated.

1. Shake Excess Water from Hands
2. Push Button
3. Massage Hands in Airstream
4. Stops Automatically!

As a sailor wets a finger and lifts it to test the wind's direction, I stepped outside and tried to gauge the drift of the craic, if any. I followed the main road to a bridge over the Clodiagh River, glittery even in the drizzle, that led to M.D. Hickey, a tidy white house with red window sashes. The house looked so private I almost knocked before I entered, but I could hear the faintest trace of voices, so I threw open the door and felt not unlike Synge's playboy when he bursts into the shebeen. A near-capacity crowd of four—two men and two women—was gathered in a front room only slightly bigger than a walk-in closet. They fell silent when they saw me—an unfamiliar face, an apparition—but that only lasted for a second before they were swept up in great swell of hospitality, waving and shouting for me to come in, come in, as if to rescue me from the night and its terrors.

At first I wondered if I actually could fit inside, but I managed to squeeze onto the fifth and last stool, where I was promptly clapped on the back by a mechanic from the village garage, who had a beaming face and a broad-beamed body. "Good man, good man!" he cried when I took a sip of my Guinness and passed over some money to an elderly woman. This was Mary Hickey, who was petite, sweet-natured, and bright-eyed, and wore her hair in a flattering permanent. She was dressed so meticulously that she might have had a Sunday school class to teach rather than a pub to run, the very archetype of a beloved grannie. If she'd brought me a plate of chocolate chip cookies with my pint, I wouldn't have blinked.

Mary had been born in the house, and she still lived there. She opened the pub around eleven thirty most mornings whether or not she had a customer, because she couldn't stop herself. The force of habit was too strong to overcome, she told me. (When I mentioned the O'Connors' failed stab at retirement to her, she laughed and exclaimed, "Go on!") Between orders, she rested in a chair and sat there like a muse, arbitrating any differences of opinion and contributing her own when appropriate. She seemed to float in and out of the talk, and sometimes retreated into a private space that her guests—I'd begun to think of us that way—respected. It was extraordinary that she could handle Hickey's on her own, without any support at all. Clonaslee and the Slieve Blooms were still so benign, apparently, that she didn't feel vulnerable.

I saw what looked like a closet door at the end of the bar. Could it really be a closet? When I opened it, I anticipated a heady whiff of mothballs, but it led to a second room, where a solitary man sat by a coal fire, absorbed in thought and soaking up the heat. The pub had a third room, too, which Mary used for storage, chiefly of a dusty upright piano whose keys sounded only four notes in tune. "I should get it fixed," she said wistfully, but she had more important repairs on her list. In such an old house, the repairs would stack up like cordwood. Her regulars once played the piano and sang, she recalled, but Clonaslee had been thriving then, and the workers from the peat bogs had money to spare.

Mary set a fresh pint in front of a man spackled everywhere with flakes of plaster. He had plaster in his hair, sprinkled on his cheeks, and powdered over his clothes and shoes. "I'm a builder," he announced happily, as though I'd never guess. Mary returned to her chair and puzzled over a leaflet that came with her new blood-pressure medication until one of the women at the bar—another Mary, a nurse from Dublin home for a visit—took it from her and translated the legalese, writing down the significant points on a napkin. She and her friend were protective toward Mary Hickey and helped with the chores, collecting the empty glasses and spreading around fresh coasters. I'd never been in a less commercial establishment. The money, though present, was incidental to the camaraderie.

Even the mechanic was proud of the pub—of belonging to its charmed circle—and he whispered to me, as if to divulge a secret, "Hickey's is very special, you know." The builder raised his glass to second the motion, while Mary, the nurse, endorsed it, too. Feisty and intelligent, she gossiped with her friend about their old school classmates, charting the rise and fall of reputations, but it made her uncomfortable to leave me out. Her nature demanded inclusion, so she'd switch to a more universal, less personal topic—the hiking trails in the mountains, say, or the beauty of the waterfalls in spring.

We talked freely, sudden intimates in the crowded front room, and though everyone's tongue was lubricated, no one acted ornery or caused any offense. To misbehave in Mary Hickey's parlor would be worse than offending Jack Birchall.

The mechanic had no opinion on the hiking trails or the waterfalls, but he conversed brilliantly about the intricacies of sparkplugs and pistons, with a poetic intensity. If my car had needed a valve job, I'd gladly have entrusted it to him. The room was awash in trust, in fact, warm to the core from a mutually generated heat. I thought about ghost stories again and sensed that our gathering recaptured the spirit and flavor of thousands of other gatherings at Hickey's over the years. The ease we felt with each other, the simplicity of our communing, they were informed by what had preceded us—so many lives and so much history, to cast it in Berger's terms. As closing time drew near, I was reluctant to go, aware that the fragile bonds of an evening would be broken, but I finally put on my coat. "Thanks for calling by," Mary Hickey said, as if we'd known each other forever.

Chapter 12

JOURNEY'S END

WHEN I WOKE in Clonaslee the next morning, still the only person rattling around at Blooms, I felt strangely disoriented. The village was as sleepy as ever, and I missed my comrades from M.D. Hickey, who'd returned to their usual pursuits. The mechanic was dressed in his coveralls again, while Mary had gone back to Dublin to resume her nursing duties. The pub itself looked calm and uneventful, an ordinary house once more. Mary Hickey might be in the kitchen right now, putting on the kettle for a cup of tea. My evening there took on the quality of a dream, never to be repeated. There was a time when I thought such evenings would fall my way consistently in Ireland, but I knew better now. As Eugene Kavanagh had said, "They won't miss us until we're gone."

At home in Ranelagh, I found an E-mail waiting for me. A friend in California had alerted me to the existence of the Flann O'Brien Original Irish Pub in Graz, Austria, so I could add it to my file of literary oddities. There was no end to the business of appropriating writers, apparently. Soon we'd have a Seamus Heaney Original Irish Pub somewhere, the Tara situation be damned. Even the real estate agents were getting into the act. I'd just seen an ad for a new tract in Leitrim, with an arrow indicating "the late John McGahern's house" on its outskirts. At any rate, Flann O'Brien probably deserved some recognition abroad, since he'd been so neglected in Dublin—no portrait at McDaids, for instance, despite his considerable patronage.

On a whim, I checked O'Brien's Web site. (There's also a Flann O'Brien's in greater Boston, I discovered.) The copywriters had done a terrific job of articulating the Irish Pub Concept's formula. It was no surprise that O'Brien's "like its namesake tries to embody this spirit"—of "Irishness," one assumes—nor was I shocked to hear that the pub had been "built on the Emerald Isle by the finest craftsmen" and shipped to Austria piece by piece. The next two sentences stopped me cold, though, because they were so wrongheaded. "Although Ireland has become a young, vibrant, energetic country in recent years [true], she is still firmly rooted in her culture and tradition [half true, at best]. In Ireland, the pub is still the focal point of every community every night [totally false]."

There was no end to the appeal of Fairytale Ireland, either, it seemed. In the pub game, the authentically replicated had trounced the authentic for the moment in spite of Walter Benjamin's assertions. For every rural pub that died, an IPC-type pub was busy being born in a foreign country, at the identical rate of one a day. The ironies didn't stop there. If an investor were to stray from the formula and reproduce a pub such as M.D. Hickey, even installing a sweetheart of a grannie to pose as Mary, most people would give it a pass in favor of Nine Fine Irishmen. Worse still, when an ordinary Irish pub revamped to comply with its owner's conception of the modern, it often resembled Nine Fine Irishmen, too.

One truth was beyond the scope of irony. The traditional pub, plainly furnished, with no phony bric-a-brac, recorded music, or TV, where a genuine publican ran the show, the barmen (or women) didn't change by the week, and the locals outnumbered the tourists, was on its last legs. In effect, Ireland's pubs could be divided into three rough categories—a handful of carefully curated trophies such as James Toner and Doheny & Nesbitt that preserve an element of tradition; neighborhood bars like those in Ringsend and the Liberties, pleasant spots but not worth a special trip; and faceless corporate pubs operated strictly for profit. The trophies would probably be around forever, but the others could join the ranks of the departed at any time.

For isolated country pubs, the future looked bleaker. Frank O'Brien's in Athy, situated in a vibrant market town, could be reinvented as a museum piece like Morrissey's of Abbeyleix if the right person came along, but Mary Hickey was unlikely to turn her front room into an Internet café, nor were the O'Connors about to hire a chef to develop a dinner menu in Ballitore. (An average pub must do about 50 percent of its trade in food if it hopes to survive, says Louis Fitzgerald. Paul Stevenson of VFI, brainstorming again, pressed for innovation, "Oriental or even organic.") The elderly publicans were just locked into a routine they'd initiated a half century ago, unwilling or unable to quit. With no successors in line, the fate of their pubs would be dictated by the real estate market and the police who patrol the roads.

My journey was over at last. I knew I might stumble on another M.D. Hickey in West Cork, say, or the far reaches of Donegal, but it wouldn't alter the picture. Better to put away the notebook, park the car at the curb, and prepare for the holidays, I advised myself, and that might have worked out if I hadn't agreed to meet Moriarity, the photographer, for a pre-Christmas drink, with the proviso that there'd be no swapping of rounds. He'd moved to a small town some months ago to cut his overhead, and his visit to Dublin was a yuletide ritual that many of the Irish indulge in, off to the big city to see the lights and the decorations on Grafton and O'Connell streets. The women do some shopping, while the men refresh themselves as necessary and calculate the damage.

I got to Birchall's first. When I entered, I felt exposed rather than sheltered now, because of the new mirrors everywhere. I hadn't yet adjusted to the makeover. It was more dramatic and extensive than I had anticipated. The pub looked more spacious, and just as handsome as McSorley's—streamlined and cleared of the random junk on Jack's shelves. It looked designed, too, and all of a piece. It *flowed*, as the architects say, and the bar blended seamlessly with the lounge. Gone was the pub's cobbled-together aspect. Gone were the dated upholstery, the letter from Guide Dogs for the Blind, and the painting of swans on the Grand Canal. Instead, some pristine copper tankards hung from pegs, and there were framed rugby crests, two giant photo blowups of famous GAA teams, and three flat-screen TVs.

As hurried as ever, Frank Smyth still bounced between pubs with his speedy stutter-step, supervising Andy and Big Andy, another Chinese recruit twice the size of the original. When I asked Frank to describe the new look once, he replied, "Traditional." Jack approved of it, he said, and came by for coffee when he wasn't playing golf or traveling. The comments from the regulars had been mostly positive, according to Frank, but I took that with a grain of salt, since only a natural disaster could budge them. The staff was gearing up for the holiday crunch, two weeks of blitzkrieg partying that would fill the cash register and exhaust the dispensers of good cheer. To recuperate, Frank was taking his family to Spain in January, where he'd steer clear of the "Irish" bars and stick to tapas.

Moriarity trailed in just minutes after me. His visit had been costly so far, he reported, but he intended to shoulder the bills stoically, without complaint. He was in an expansive mood. His photo studio was doing well, thanks to the wedding portraits and such that he swore he'd never stoop to when he still viewed himself as the next Cartier-Bresson, so he was flush and delighted to treat his partner S. to a night at the august Shelbourne Hotel, recently renovated like every other entity in Dublin and part of the Marriott chain now. S. and Moriarity had been together for almost a year, but she didn't know, of course, that she'd set a record for longevity, yet it's a fact that your man cut a wide swath among the impressionable art students until he mended his ways and began the day with Barry's tea instead of stout.

Under his new program, he never touched a drop before the evening and rarely went overboard when he did, more content than ever with his work—he still took artistic photos, too—and in his relationship, a word I'd never heard him utter before except as a kind of snarl. Against the odds, Moriarity appeared to be settling down, although he showed some of his former fire when I spoke the r-word myself and asked if he was serious about S. He almost bit me, flashing his incisors at the stupidity of the question—"*Life* is serious!"—and my naïveté in putting it to him, even though he'd have done the same if the shoe had been on the other foot. Some friendships just don't abide by the rules of common sense.

What did Moriarity think of the new Birchall's? He seemed unfazed, so I prodded him. He took a minute to survey the pub, already quite busy at five in the afternoon and bubbling with a giddy energy born of blistered credit cards. "Shabbily genteel Dublin is dead," he pronounced, "and scarcely a soul will care." He among all men mourned the loss of shabby gentility, he elaborated, and its passing caused him to wax nostalgic for his days as a carouser. He remembered the curative power of an early pint at the Lord Edward, the lively patter at Grogan's, and the homey sustenance of Brogan's, all pubs I hadn't sampled.

"Never?" Moriarity questioned, an eyebrow raised.

"Ireland has about twelve thousand pubs."

"I take your point, in fairness. But still, the Lord Edward . . ."

The Irish say "in fairness" so often I'm sure they really mean the opposite. I translated Moriarity's remark as, "I'd like to be fair and honor your point, but you've committed such a colossal blunder, I can't do it"—not that he didn't bend over backward to pretend that he understood my dilemma. He carried on about how one should never interfere in somebody else's creative process, because you always sound critical even when you're being constructive, et cetera. He alluded to the "daunting logistics" I faced, too, but the knife was already in. How could I have overlooked those pubs? What if they turned out to be gems? In a flash, I went from being a confident authority to an uninformed misfit.

The irrational dotes on anxiety, and it strikes when you're feeling vulnerable. I believed I'd come to the end of the road, but Moriarity, insensitive to the extent of my efforts, able to afford a posh room in a five-star hotel with a view of Stephen's Green, had the nerve to remind me, perhaps correctly, that the road has no end. Every ending is *arbitrary*, he implied, in the same way that certain paintings are never truly completed. In *fairness*, he didn't mean any harm. He was just callous and remote in the moment. Despite his astounding lack of empathy, he must have sensed my distress, because he insisted I drop by the hotel, say hello to S., and have a nightcap.

High spirits engulfed Moriarity when we hit the streets. "This walk used to take me four hours," he laughed, talking about all the stops he once made while he covered the mile and a half to the green. First he had a pint at the Waterloo on Pembroke Road, where Jim of the Oarsmen had worked ("It's a superpub now, unfortunately.") and sometimes at Smyth's nearby (no relation to Frank), then proceeded to the Bermuda Triangle of Nesbitt's, Toner's, and O'Donaghue's on Lower Baggot Street ("Men have been sucked under there and never found again.") before he reached the grand dame of a hotel that Elizabeth Bowen called "an affair of size, ruddiness, solidarity, good-nature, prosperity, and prestige."

Martin Burke of Tipperary yoked together four brick houses to build the Shelbourne in 1824. Prior to the Marriott takeover, the hotel with its worn carpets and frumpy couches had lost its former glory and had become a candidate for shabby gentility. Disheveled poets hunkered at the elegant Horseshoe Bar, lunched on the free peanuts, and were tolerated because they behaved themselves, but they've been priced out of the market. The Shelbourne's tony again, beautifully refurbished, and very expensive. The landed gentry still employs it as a base for such special occasions as black-tie balls and deb parties, just as it did in Thackeray's time ("a respectable old edifice, much frequented by families from the country . . ."), and the hotel has a "genealogy butler" on staff to assist Irish-American guests interested in their ancestry, but it's the new-money crowd that has adopted its public rooms as a playground.

When you spin through the revolving doors that lead to the lobby, you're thrust into the midst of an ongoing celebration that seems to have begun just before your arrival, with a potpourri of people who can't wait to shake your hand and put a glass into it. The atmosphere is upbeat and frivolous, and it promotes a sense of well-being and also an inkling that you must be among the elect, an idea you'd have scoffed at if it had been proposed to you fifteen minutes earlier. There's a good bit of middle-aged cruising on the weekend nights that relies on a healthy pour of champagne—always a boon to romances with a short shelf life destined to expire no later than Sunday afternoon.

The Horseshoe Bar was too jammed to accommodate us, so we adjourned to the No. 27 Bar on the other side of the hotel, a brighter space where the elbow room was still at a premium. There are those (Moriarty) who thrive on being pressed in wafer-thin among strangers—this may be another trait of Irishness—but I'd have been overjoyed to go elsewhere, or even walk back to Birchall's. Thank goodness for S., who joined us and had a soothing effect on my overwrought state of mind. Though I was happy for my insensitive friend, who'd chosen a warm-hearted, compassionate woman at last, and thrilled to be chatting about less onerous subjects than my shortcomings, all I really wanted to do was to go home, read a book of the soporific variety, and forget about the 11,873 pubs I hadn't visited.

The approach of the holidays in Dublin gains momentum with alarming force. A week before Christmas, the downtown streets were already thick with shoppers in Santa hats, bright red with fuzzy white pompoms. Some people wore paper crowns instead, the kind that come inside a cracker along with a prize you probably never dreamed of owning—a midget screwdriver, say, or a little plastic whistle. The crackers were featured at the office lunches that spilled out over tables heavily laden with wine. Nobody went back to work after eating, of course. It was too late in the day and almost dark, the indigo sky pinpricked with stars, and invariably someone who knew what lay ahead—a headache when the wine wore off, a furry mouth, and a dozen packages to wrap—voted to postpone it by asking, "Stop at the pub?"

An amusing story was going around the pubs that December. It concerned some scientists at the University of Wisconsin, whose research showed that Guinness, taken in a twenty-four-ounce measure with a meal, might be as effective as low-dose aspirin in preventing blood clots and staving off heart attacks. Lager doesn't have the same potential, perhaps because it lacks the antioxidants—or so the scientists surmised—but other experts argued that alcohol in any form has properties that inhibit clotting. The news sounded promising, at any rate, until you learned that the test subjects were dogs with narrowed arteries. Dubliners are quick to seize on any aspect of the ridiculous, so there were the inevitable jokes about ordering a bowl of stout rather than a pint.

I heard the joke in Brogan's on Dame Street. I'd gone there for a specific reason, so that Moriarity wouldn't get the better of me. Obviously, I'd miss some fine traditional pubs in Ireland—I'd known that from the outset!—but at least they wouldn't be the ones my friend had pined for in his theatrical way. My honest hope was that all three of his suggestions would be losers, but Brogan's looked like a contender. For starters, there was the photo in the front window. It showed Ginger, an undefeated fighting cock and the All-Ireland Heavyweight Champion, sipping his "second pint" with Dennis Hyland, a human being, in 1960. Ginger's beak and half his crimson head were buried in the foam, and an empty glass by his right claw "proved" that it wasn't his first.

Brogan's also earned a good grade for being so basic, as dull inside as it was without. The pub scored another point for its little upholstered stools reminiscent of the old Birchall's, but the walls were an eyesore, so plastered with ads and posters for Guinness I was reminded of the roadside shrines in Mexico that peasants assemble from scraps of votive material. (St. James's Gate was suspiciously close by, in fact.) The ads often centered on the Guinness toucan—an avian theme was developing here—introduced as a corporate symbol in 1935. The first ad of the campaign pictured the toucan with two pints of stout, perhaps the medically approved dosage for birds to judge by Ginger. The author of the accompanying jingle was Dorothy L. Sayers, later a distinguished writer of mysteries.

> If he can say as you can
> Guinness is good for you
> How grand to be a Toucan
> Just think what two can do

It's possible the ads were originals, not repros, and had some historical value, but I tended to think otherwise. A TV was on at Brogan's, too, recycling Sky News as usual, so I relegated the pub to the category of a neighborhood bar—a homey one, it's true, but hardly deserving Moriarty's exaggerated praise. Next I tried the Lord Edward near Christ Church Cathedral, a short stroll away. The pub is easily recognizable because of the portrait of Lord Edward Fitzgerald on the front of the building, a dashing youth in a green frock coat and a red cravat. Fitzgerald, the fifth son of the Duke of Leinster, was a rebel nationalist. He died in a shootout with British troops, while he hid at a house in the Liberties that belonged to a dealer in feathers.

The Lord Edward is also the oldest seafood restaurant in Dublin, and the laminated menu posted outside offers ample clues to the cuisine—Sole Meuniere, Lobster Newburg, Scallops St. Jacques, here were the very classics Fitzgerald might have dined on himself before his death in 1798. The pub spread itself over two floors, with a lounge above the bar. The lounge, very spare, had some tables crafted from wine barrels and more portraits of the lord. The bar below, another horseshoe like the Shelbourne's, was small and well attended by the locals, who were served the same portion of Sky News available at Brogan's.

Two down and one to go. I couldn't wait to be done with my tour. As difficult as it is to believe, I was losing my appetite for pubs, much like a man who declares his undying affection for T-bone steak and then is force-fed it for the rest of his life. Pubs had also begun to affect my dreams, and not in a healthy way. In one nightmare, a Poe derivative, I was locked in a cellar full of kegs after closing time. Only the desire to upbraid Moriarty propelled me toward Grogan's—the Castle Lounge J. Grogan, more accurately. If you had warned me months ago, when the Brazen Head was still virgin territory, that I'd someday almost not want a pint of Guinness, I would have laughed, but the day had come.

Grogan's location confirmed its status as a trophy. It's just off Grafton Street and adjacent to Powerscourt Townhouse, a shopping complex and formerly the urban retreat of Richard Wingfield, the viscount of Powerscourt. Wingfield had a vast estate in Enniskerry, County Wicklow, whose architect was Richard Castle. That could account for the Castle Lounge tag, although nearby Dublin Castle, once billed as "the worst castle in the worst situation in Christendom," could explain it, as well. The pub's exterior was lackluster and no different from so many others in town, with its name in simple block letters and no additional adornments. Inside I expected to find a few ragged diehards waiting out the typical doldrums of the late afternoon, but Grogan's was jam-packed at 4:43 P.M.

Even in the depths of winter, its two little rooms were so steamy with body heat that a barman had switched on a fan to keep from breaking a sweat. There must have been fifty drinkers in the pub, but not one was gaping at Sky News. Grogan's doesn't have a television, nor does it inflict any recorded music on its clientele. It isn't an old pub by Dublin's hoary standards, with just fifty years or so of business under its belt, and it's furnished with the sort of tatty tables and chairs you see in the flats of graduate students still disengaged from the idea of earning a living. Its only eye-catching attribute is the ongoing exhibition of art on the walls—figurative paintings, mostly, in a wide range of styles from the tortured threnody of Munch and Nolde to the peaceful Constable pastoral. There was even a portrait of James Dean, although not on black velvet.

I scanned the walls for a Moriarity, perhaps a nude study from his raffish period, but his work wasn't on display. That didn't mean he hadn't hocked a photo for drinks in the past, though, because the art at Grogan's can be purchased and a Moriarity nude might have sold, although my guess was that the regulars were liable to spend their cash on pints rather than pictures. Be that as it may, the pub was such a winner that my appetite for Guinness returned, and while Tommy Smith, who owns Grogan's with a partner, tended to the stout, I marveled at the mixed batch of customers—Trinity students, businessmen, and aging bohos—all talking and drinking in what amounted to a fine democracy of the spirit.

At Grogan's, you can help yourself to a stack of papers and magazines, a mini-library free for the asking. Better still, you can assuage your hunger with a toasted sandwich prepared to order, not wrapped in cellophane in advance. It did my heart good to spot a toaster on a shelf of the bar, just like the one Jack Birchall used. A second barman, who was learning the trade under Tommy's patient tutelage, applied some butter to the bread, then laid on the ham and cheese. That was enough to endear Grogan's to me for life, although the pub had a topper in store. The sandwich came with a proper jar of Colman's Mustard, rather that the usual selection of condiments in plastic packets.

I ordered a toastie myself. Why not? Christmas was in the wings. As much as I hated to admit it, Moriarity had steered me right on Grogan's, although he was only one for three in the recommendation department, a statistic I'd file away for future reference and debate. Grogan's qualified as a true traditional pub, surely among the best in the city when you factored in the talk, which was a cut above the average, wide-ranging and discriminating. I conversed with a Trinity lad who was a fan of Raymond Carver's stories, and we compared our favorites and moved on to the King George steeplechase to be run in England on Stephen's Day. The time passed without my taking any notice of it, another felicitous aspect of being in the right place.

For the holidays, Kevin Hynes wrapped McSorley & Sons in a big red ribbon with a fulsome bow, as if the delights of the season were concealed inside. At Birchall's, Frank Smyth settled for a subdued array of ornaments and tinsel, but those outpourings, however generous and good-willed, weren't really necessary to remind the regulars Christmas had almost arrived. They already knew that the ordinary rules had been suspended. A pint was permissible at any hour, because Dublin itself was on the nod, virtually shut down until the second week of January. The postmen, the librarians, the bureaucrats in the city offices by Merchants Quay, they'd clock in only as necessary, doing their best to ignore any obligation that might interrupt the flow of the craic.

On Christmas Eve, I returned from a last-minute shopping trip with my blistered credit card in hand and rolled into Birchall's, but I could barely make it to the bar, so dense was the traffic at seven o'clock. The same lemming-like rush was probably going on at the Flann O'Brien in Graz—and at the Blarney Stone in Tokyo and Finnegan's Irish Pub in Rome—as merrymakers gravitated toward the gentler, uncomplicated, fun-filled world of Fairytale Ireland. In real Ireland, the crush had its roots in the sad fact that the pubs wouldn't be open on Christmas Day, at least not legally, although some publicans were known to take pity on the wounded. As John B. Keane put it, "They proffered the excuse that they could not bear to see so many downcast souls suffering untreated hangovers wandering the streets and laneways without a hope of recovery."

As a publican in Kerry, Keane had acquired the knack of keeping the coppers at bay. To protect his after-hours drinkers on Sunday nights, he hired Jimmy Joy as his lookout, a "brilliant exponent of the little-known art." Keane's customers entered by a back door, and alerted Jimmy with a special knock—a rap, a pause, and two more raps. Jimmy ducked down to peek through a crack, and checked the supplicant's shoes. If they were brown, the supplicant gained admission, because the police never wore brown shoes on duty. A pair of black shoes raised a question mark, and Jimmy would eyeball the trousers for creases. The policemen's trousers weren't ironed, it seems, so the door remained shut.

On the dangers of spirits, Keane was equally sound. "If a man tells you he has mastered whiskey, you can be certain that is the whiskey talking," he wrote. I indulged in a tot myself on Stephen's Day, careful as I lifted the bottle of Jameson not to overdo it and begin the slow descent into the dram drinker's madness of yore. I watched the great chaser Kauto Star fly over the fences at Kempton Park to win the King George in a breeze, after which I limped toward New Year's Eve with the rest of the country, determined to stay home and avoid the ruckus of "amateur night," as Moriarity calls it. A few days later, the *Irish Independent* ran a front-page story on the death of the pub—the good ones, anyway, "killed off by blaring music, multiple TVs, and third-rate soccer."

That wasn't news to me, of course, but the story was actually much more complicated. It was about the potential impact on Ireland's "historic identity," and about the decline of the Irish village, where those generic logos of franchises were replacing the distinctive shopfronts. It was about the vanishing greenbelt, too, and the farmers' struggle to survive, and also about the new suburbs that were being built without much planning. It was about values, as well, and money and a highway that threatened Tara—about the rapidity of change and the problems that come with it.

For the Irish, the revelry draws to a close on Epiphany, January sixth, known as *Nollaig Bheag*, or Little Christmas, and also as Women's Christmas, a day when men are supposed to discharge the household chores and then make themselves scarce, while their wives, girlfriends, mothers, aunties, and so on gather to do whatever it is they do. I'd laid in the provisions for dinner, so I had only to become invisible, an easy enough job. I slipped from the house before the guests arrived and walked to the city center once again, around Christ Church, past the Brazen Head, and over Father Mathew Bridge to Smithfield, where all manner of activity was going on.

At one end of the square, a skating rink had been set up— Dublin on Ice, an annual extravaganza. Everywhere kids were clamoring for skates, or inspecting the bruises they'd gotten after renting a pair and taking a fall. At the other end, the last stragglers from the Sunday horse fair were leading away their bedraggled animals. A pony boy in a track suit leaped onto his mount, a sorry-looking creature shedding its hair in clumps, and dug in his heels and rode off like a prince of the city, cars and buses be damned. Nearby, a traveler and his son were trying to induce their horse, an Irish cob, to go forward rather than stand still. They slapped its hindquarters, yanked on the bridle, and bellowed in its ears until the horse obeyed.

The ancient cobbles of Smithfield were thick with steaming manure, and smeared with it where the unwary had planted a foot by mistake. Though some believe this brings good luck, I preferred no luck at all and watched my step on the way to the Cobblestone, where a drop-in session was about to begin. Mick, the flute player, was at its center again, a robust anchor for three fiddles, a second flute, and a tin whistle. In the delicate half-light of winter, I sat at the bar with my Guinness, thoroughly content and remembering Eugene Kavanagh's line once more. About the time when pistachio oil reaches Ireland's farthest outposts—a hamlet on the Beara Peninsula, say, where the fishermen still mend their nets—people might look up forlornly and recall the simple pleasure of a pint of plain.

How odd it was to consider that Fairytale Ireland, where Finian's rainbow dispels the gloom and Sean Thornton still lives at White O'Mornin', had been concocted in part from the virtues that the traditional pub embodies—civility and kindness, warmth and good humor, a love of talk and a sense of community, all those qualities I'd felt and been nourished by at M.D. Hickey, where I'd been rescued from the night. Almost everywhere, the local—as in the particular, the unique—was under siege, batted about the head by the insistently global. I had nothing against Gourmet Burger and might even eat there soon—and probably enjoy it—but I'd go to the Gravediggers to touch the soul of Ireland.

The soul of Ireland was far too weighty a topic for the Cobblestone, though, and I already knew myself to be in its presence, anyway, as I happily hoisted a glass. The scene couldn't be manufactured or authentically replicated anywhere else on earth, and therein lay its beauty. As I floated along with the music, I wondered what had happened to Derek, the minstrel lad with the red button accordion. I hoped his Christmas had been bountiful, and that he hadn't been kidnapped again by the same gang of friends who'd dragged him from pub to pub until his pockets were almost empty—or if he *had* been kidnapped that he played his squeeze-box with a celestial fire, but here the fiddles interrupted my meditation and rose to a crescendo that broke like a wave, and all fell silent again. I took a breath and a sip of stout. I felt relaxed, uplifted. As for ordinary cares, I had none.

ACKNOWLEDGMENTS

My thanks to Donall O'Keefe, the chief executive of the Licensed Vintners Association, for the useful information he supplied on the pub trade in Dublin, and to Noel Darby of the Irish Pub Company for his insights into its operation. I am grateful, as well, to the Traditional Music Archive and the National Library, where the staff members were unfailingly helpful with my research. I am indebted, of course, to the publicans who were willing to talk with and educate me about a trade more mysterious than one might assume. George Gibson and Michele Amundsen offered kind editorial advice, and Liz Darhansoff, my agent, her much-appreciated support.

Among my bibliographic sources, I must single out in particular Cian Molloy's *The Story of the Irish Pub*, a fine introduction to the territory I explored; the oral histories of Kevin Kearns, invaluable to anyone who hopes to understand bedrock Dublin; Anthony Cronin's incisive, beautifully written *Dead as Doornails* for its unsparing account of McDaids during its literary heyday; and *Brewer's Dictionary of Irish Phrase and Fable*, compiled by Sean McMahon and Jo O'Donoghue, for the many leads and clues it provided.

Pubs differ in their approach to the apostrophe, as noted in the text. O'Donoghue's uses it, for example, while Russells doesn't. I have translated euros into dollars as necessary, but the exchange rate is volatile these days, so the figures should be taken as rough estimates only.

BIBLIOGRAPHY

Behan, Brian, and Aubrey Dillon-Malone. *The Brothers Behan*. Dublin: Ashfield Press, 1998.

Bowen, Elizabeth. *The Shelbourne*. London: Vintage Classics, 2001.

Brady, Ciaran, ed. *The Hutchison Encyclopedia of Ireland*. Oxford: Helicon, 2000.

Carson, Ciaran. *Last Night's Fun*. London: Jonathan Cape, 1996.

———. *The Pocket Guide to Traditional Music*. Belfast: Appletree Press, 1986.

Cheng, Vincent J. *Inauthentic: The Anxiety Over Culture and Indentity*. New Brunswick, NJ: Rutgers University Press, 2004.

Costello, Peter. *Dublin's Literary Pubs*. Dublin: A. & A. Farmer, 1998.

Court, Artelia. *Puck of the Droms*. Berkeley: University of California Press, 1985.

Cronin, Anthony. *Dead as Doornails*. Dublin: Poolbeg Press, 1980.

Davis, John, ed. *Rural Change in Ireland*. Belfast: Queens University Press, 1999.

Deery, Oisin. *A Compact History of Birr*. Birr: Tama Books, 2001.

Fagan, Terry. *Monto: Madams, Murder, and Black Coddle*. Dublin: North Inner City Folklore Project, 2002.

Feehan, John, ed. *Farming in Ireland*. Dublin: University College Dublin, 2003.

Ferriter, Diarmand. *A Nation of Extremes: The Pioneers in Twentieth Century Ireland*. Dublin: Irish Academic Press, 1999.

Flynn, Arthur. *Ringsend and Her Sister Villages*. Dublin: Anna Livia Press, 1990.

Gibbon, Luke. *The Quiet Man*. Cork: Cork University Press, 2002.

Grayson, Kent, and Radan Martinec. "Consumer Perception of Iconicity and Indexicality and Their Influence on Assessments of Authentic Market Offerings." *Journal of Consumer Research* 31, 2 (September 2004): 296–312.

Guinness, Arthur Son & Co. *The Guinness Brewery: St. James's Gate.* Dublin: Arthur Guinness Son & Co., 1994.

Guinness, Jonathan. *Requiem for a Family Business.* London: Macmillan, 1996.

Haliday, Charles. *An Inquiry Into the Influence of Spiritous Liquors.* Dublin: Richard Milliken & Son, 1830.

Healy, James N. *Ballads from the Pubs of Ireland.* Cork: Mercier Press, 1996.

Hughes, David. *A Bottle of Guinness, Please.* Berkshire: Phimory, 2006.

Inglis, Tom. *Moral Monopoly: The Rise and Fall of the Catholic Church in Modern Ireland.* Dublin: University College Press, 1998.

Kavanagh, Patrick. *Collected Poems.* New York: W. W. Norton, 1964.

Keane, John B. *Irish Stories for Christmas.* Boulder, Col.: Roberts Rinehart, 1994.

———. *Self-Portrait.* Dublin: Mercier Press, 1964.

Kearns, Kevin C. *Dublin Pub Life and Lore.* Dublin: Gill & Macmillan, 1996.

———. *Dublin Tenement Life.* Dublin: Gill & Macmillan, 1996.

———. *Streets Broad and Narrow: Images of Vanishing Dublin.* Dublin: Gill & Macmillan, 2000.

Kelly, Deidre. *Four Roads to Dublin.* Dublin: O'Brien, 1995.

Kenny, David. *Erendipity: The Irish Miscellany.* Dublin: Mentor Books, 2006.

Kenny, Fearga. *Jip-Cat, Pig's Head, Petticoats, and Combinations.* Tullamore: Tullamore Active Retirement, 2000.

Leadbeater, Mary. *The Leadbeater Papers,* volume I. London: Routledge/Thoenemes Press, 1999.

MacLysaght, Edward. *Irish Life in the Seventeenth Century.* Cork: Cork University Press, 1950.

Malcolm, Elizabeth. *Ireland Sober, Ireland Free: Drink and Temperance in Nineteenth Century Ireland.* Dublin: Gill & Macmillan, 1986.

Malone, Aubrey. *Historic Pubs of Dublin.* Dublin: New Island, 2001.

McBride, Joseph. *Searching for John Ford.* London: Faber and Faber, 2003.

McGowan, Joe. *In the Shadow of Benbulben.* Leitrim: Drumlin Publishers, 1993.

McKenna, Denis, ed. *A Local History of Sandymount, Irishtown, and Ringsend*. Dublin: Sandymount Community Services, 1993.

———. *The Roads to Sandymount, Irishtown, and Ringsend*. Dublin: Sandymount Community Services, 1996.

McMahon, Sean, and Jo O'Donoghue. *Brewer's Dictionary of Irish Phrase and Fable*. London: Weidenfeld & Nicolson, 2004.

McNee, Gerald. *In the Footsteps of the Quiet Man*. Edinburgh: Mainstream, 1990.

McPherson, Conor. *The Weir*. London: Nick Hern, 1998.

Molloy, Cian. *The Story of the Irish Pub*. Dublin: Liffey Press, 2002.

Murphy, J. J. *Guide to the Quiet Man*. Cong: n.d.

Negra, Diane, ed. *The Irish in Us*. Durham: Duke University Press, 2006.

O'Brien, Edna. *Mother Ireland*. London: Penguin Books, 1976.

O'Gorman, Andrew. *A Handbook for the Licensed Trade*. Dublin: A. O'Gorman, 1994.

O'Keefe, Phil. *Down Cobbled Streets: A Liberties Childhood*. Dublin: Dingle Brandon, 1995.

O'Neill, Francis. *Irish Folk Music: A Fascinating Hobby*. Chicago: Regan Print House, 1910.

———. *Irish Minstrels and Musicians*. Dublin: Mercier Press Ltd., 1987. (reprint).

———. *O'Neill's Music of Ireland: Eight Hundred and Fifty Melodies*. Chicago: Lyon & Healy, 1908.

Payne, Greg, ed. *History of Sandymount, Irishtown, and Ringsend*. Sandymount Community Services, 1989.

Peace, Adrian. *A World of Fine Difference: The Social Architecture of a Modern Irish Village*. Dublin: University College Press, 2001.

Petrie, George. *The Petrie Collection of the Ancient Music of Ireland*. London: Gregg International, 1969.

Purcell, Mary. *Remembering Matt Talbot*. Dublin: Veritas, 1954.

St. Andrew's Heritage Project. *Along the Quays and Cobblestones*. Dublin: St. Andrew's Heritage Project, 1992.

Share, Perry. "A Genuine 'Third Place'? Toward an Understanding of the Pub in Contemporary Irish Society." Thirtieth SAI Annual Conference, Cavan, 2003.

Somerville-Large, Peter. *Dublin*. London: Hamish Hamilton, 1979.

Stivers, Richard. *Hair of the Dog.* New York: Continuum, 2000.

Synge, John Millington. *The Aran Islands.* London: Penguin Books, 1992.

Taaffe, Frank. *Eye On Athy's Past.* Athy: Ardreigh Press, 2000.

Townend, Paul A. *Father Mathew, Temperance, and Irish Identity.* Portland: Irish Academic Press, 2002.

Trodd, Valentine. *Midlanders.* Banagher: Sceal Publications, 1994.

Wallis, Geoff, and Sue Wilson. *Rough Guide to Irish Music.* London: Rough Guides Ltd., 2000.

Wilson, Derek. *Dark and Light: The Story of the Guinness Family.* London: Orion, 1999.

Young, Arthur. *A Tour in Ireland.* Belfast: Blackstaff, 1983.